Copyright © 2020 by Happy Turtle Press

All rights reserved.

No part of this book may be reproduced in any form or by any electronic or mechanical means, including information storage and retrieval systems, without written permission from the author, except for the use of brief quotations in a book review.

A) Solve.

hot dog = $1.20	cola = $1.30
order of French-fries = $1.20	ice cream cone = $1.40
hamburger = $2.10	milk shake = $2.10
deluxe cheeseburger = $3.00	taco = $2.60

1) _____ Jackie wants to buy a deluxe cheeseburger, a hot dog, and a taco. How much will it cost her?

2) _____ Steven wants to buy a hamburger. How much will he have to pay?

3) _____ If Sandra buys a deluxe cheeseburger, an ice cream cone, and a cola, and if she had $20.00, how much money will she have left?

4) _____ Adam purchases a hamburger, a milk shake, and an order of French-fries. How much money will he get back if he pays $20.00?

5) _____ If Jake buys an ice cream cone, a hamburger, and a hot dog, what will his change be if he pays $10.00?

6) _____ What is the total cost of a cola and a hamburger if the sales tax is 5%?

7) _____ If Allan buys a taco, a deluxe cheeseburger, and a hamburger, how much change will he get back from $20.00?

8) _____ Brian purchases an ice cream cone. How much change will he get back from $10.00?

9) _____ If Ellen buys a taco, and if she had $10.00, how much money will she have left?

10) _____ Michele purchases a cola and a taco. How much change will she get back from $10.00?

B) Solve.

hot dog = $1.00	cola = $1.40
order of French-fries = $0.80	ice cream cone = $1.20
hamburger = $2.60	milk shake = $2.10
deluxe cheeseburger = $3.30	taco = $2.50

1) _____ What is the total cost of a deluxe cheeseburger, a milk shake, and a hamburger if there is a five percent sales tax?

2) _____ If David buys a cola, how much change will he get back from $10.00?

3) _____ What is the total cost of a cola and a taco if there is a five percent sales tax?

4) _____ What is the total cost of a milk shake, a hamburger, and a cola if there is a 5% sales tax?

5) _____ What is the total cost of a milk shake, an ice cream cone, and a cola?

6) _____ What is the total cost of a cola and a deluxe cheeseburger if there is a five percent sales tax?

7) _____ Jake wants to buy a milk shake, an order of French-fries, and a hamburger. How much will he have to pay?

8) _____ If Steven wanted to buy an ice cream cone and a cola, how much would it cost him?

9) _____ What is the total cost of an order of French-fries, a milk shake, and an ice cream cone?

10) _____ If Ellen buys a milk shake, and if she had $5.00, how much money will she have left?

C) Solve.

hot dog = $1.60	cola = $1.20
order of French-fries = $0.90	ice cream cone = $1.00
hamburger = $2.60	milk shake = $2.80
deluxe cheeseburger = $3.50	taco = $2.10

1) _____ If Jackie wanted to buy an order of French-fries, how much money would she need?

2) _____ What is the total cost of a milk shake and a taco?

3) _____ If Sharon wanted to buy an ice cream cone and an order of French-fries, how much would she have to pay?

4) _____ Donald purchases a taco, a milk shake, and a hot dog. How much money will he get back if he pays $10.00?

5) _____ If Jake wanted to buy an order of French-fries, a cola, and a milk shake, how much money would he need?

6) _____ If Marin wanted to buy an ice cream cone, a taco, and a cola, how much would she have to pay?

7) _____ If Michele wanted to buy a cola, a deluxe cheeseburger, and a taco, how much would it cost her?

8) _____ Sandra purchases an order of French-fries, a cola, and a taco. How much money will she get back if she pays $10.00?

9) _____ Jennifer purchases a cola and an ice cream cone. If she had $10.00, how much money will she have left?

10) _____ What is the total cost of a hot dog and an order of French-fries?

Happy Turtle Press   Shopping Problems

D) Solve.

hot dog = $1.60	cola = $1.10
order of French-fries = $0.70	ice cream cone = $1.90
hamburger = $2.80	milk shake = $2.00
deluxe cheeseburger = $3.70	taco = $2.90

1) _____ Sandra wants to buy a hot dog. How much will it cost her?

2) _____ Jackie purchases a cola and a deluxe cheeseburger. How much change will she get back from $10.00?

3) _____ David purchases a cola, an ice cream cone, and a taco. If he had $20.00, how much money will he have left?

4) _____ What is the total cost of a hot dog if there is a five percent sales tax?

5) _____ What is the total cost of a hamburger and a taco if the sales tax is five percent?

6) _____ If Donald wanted to buy a cola and a milk shake, how much would he have to pay?

7) _____ What is the total cost of a deluxe cheeseburger, a taco, and an ice cream cone if the sales tax is five percent?

8) _____ Billy wants to buy an order of French-fries and a cola. How much money will he need?

9) _____ Marin purchases a taco. How much change will she get back from $10.00?

10) _____ If Paul wanted to buy a cola, an order of French-fries, and a taco, how much would he have to pay?

E) Solve.

hot dog = $1.30	cola = $1.30
order of French-fries = $0.80	ice cream cone = $1.90
hamburger = $2.00	milk shake = $2.50
deluxe cheeseburger = $3.90	taco = $2.40

1) _____ If Audrey buys a hamburger, an ice cream cone, and a cola, and if she had $20.00, how much money will she have left?

2) _____ Michele purchases a deluxe cheeseburger, a hamburger, and a milk shake. How much change will she get back from $20.00?

3) _____ Adam wants to buy a cola and a taco. How much money will he need?

4) _____ If Ellen wanted to buy a hamburger, how much money would she need?

5) _____ Jennifer wants to buy an ice cream cone. How much money will she need?

6) _____ What is the total cost of a milk shake, an ice cream cone, and an order of French-fries?

7) _____ If Sharon wanted to buy a deluxe cheeseburger and a hot dog, how much money would she need?

8) _____ Jackie purchases a milk shake and a hot dog. If she had $10.00, how much money will she have left?

9) _____ Allan purchases an order of French-fries and a taco. How much money will he get back if he pays $10.00?

10) _____ What is the total cost of a deluxe cheeseburger, a hot dog, and a milk shake if the sales tax is 5%?

F) Solve.

hot dog = $1.40	cola = $1.10
order of French-fries = $0.80	ice cream cone = $1.20
hamburger = $2.80	milk shake = $2.00
deluxe cheeseburger = $3.60	taco = $2.40

1) _____ Sandra wants to buy a cola, a milk shake, and an ice cream cone. How much money will she need?

2) _____ Allan wants to buy a hot dog, a milk shake, and a taco. How much money will he need?

3) _____ Audrey purchases a hamburger and a cola. What will her change be if she pays $10.00?

4) _____ What is the total cost of a cola and an order of French-fries if the sales tax is 5%?

5) _____ What is the total cost of a taco and an ice cream cone if there is a five percent sales tax?

6) _____ If Jake wanted to buy an ice cream cone and a milk shake, how much would it cost him?

7) _____ Jennifer purchases a deluxe cheeseburger and an order of French-fries. How much change will she get back from $10.00?

8) _____ Donald wants to buy a taco and a hamburger. How much will it cost him?

9) _____ Janet purchases a cola. What will her change be if she pays $5.00?

10) _____ If Ellen buys a hot dog, a taco, and a milk shake, and if she had $10.00, how much money will she have left?

G) Solve.

hot dog = $1.00	cola = $1.10
order of French-fries = $1.30	ice cream cone = $1.10
hamburger = $2.10	milk shake = $2.10
deluxe cheeseburger = $3.90	taco = $2.20

1) _____ What is the total cost of an ice cream cone?

2) _____ If Donald buys a taco and a deluxe cheeseburger, and if he had $20.00, how much money will he have left?

3) _____ If Michele wanted to buy a hamburger and an ice cream cone, how much money would she need?

4) _____ If Marcie buys a hamburger, an ice cream cone, and a deluxe cheeseburger, how much money will she get back if she pays $10.00?

5) _____ What is the total cost of a hot dog if there is a 5% sales tax?

6) _____ What is the total cost of an ice cream cone and a milk shake?

7) _____ What is the total cost of a cola and a hot dog if there is a 5% sales tax?

8) _____ Audrey purchases a hot dog. If she had $5.00, how much money will she have left?

9) _____ Janet purchases a taco. How much money will she get back if she pays $5.00?

10) _____ What is the total cost of an ice cream cone, an order of French-fries, and a hamburger if the sales tax is 5%?

H) Solve.

hot dog = $1.00	cola = $1.00
order of French-fries = $0.80	ice cream cone = $1.10
hamburger = $2.90	milk shake = $2.20
deluxe cheeseburger = $3.70	taco = $3.00

1) _____ What is the total cost of a milk shake, an order of French-fries, and a hot dog?

2) _____ Jennifer wants to buy a milk shake and a deluxe cheeseburger. How much money will she need?

3) _____ If Paul wanted to buy a deluxe cheeseburger, how much money would he need?

4) _____ If Ellen buys an order of French-fries and a hamburger, how much change will she get back from $10.00?

5) _____ If Jackie buys an order of French-fries, how much change will she get back from $10.00?

6) _____ Amy purchases an order of French-fries, a taco, and a hot dog. If she had $10.00, how much money will she have left?

7) _____ Billy wants to buy an ice cream cone and an order of French-fries. How much money will he need?

8) _____ Allan wants to buy a milk shake and a hamburger. How much will it cost him?

9) _____ If David wanted to buy a milk shake, how much would it cost him?

10) _____ If Marcie wanted to buy an order of French-fries, how much would she have to pay?

I) Solve.

hot dog = $1.30	cola = $1.30
order of French-fries = $1.20	ice cream cone = $1.60
hamburger = $2.20	milk shake = $2.10
deluxe cheeseburger = $3.00	taco = $2.00

1) _____ Jackie wants to buy a hamburger. How much will it cost her?

2) _____ If Amy wanted to buy an ice cream cone and a hamburger, how much would it cost her?

3) _____ Michele wants to buy a cola, a hot dog, and an order of French-fries. How much will she have to pay?

4) _____ If Ellen buys a taco and a cola, and if she had $10.00, how much money will she have left?

5) _____ If Marin wanted to buy an ice cream cone, a deluxe cheeseburger, and a cola, how much would she have to pay?

6) _____ What is the total cost of a deluxe cheeseburger and a milk shake?

7) _____ If Billy wanted to buy a taco and a hamburger, how much money would he need?

8) _____ Sandra wants to buy a hot dog, a milk shake, and a taco. How much money will she need?

9) _____ Jake purchases a hot dog, a taco, and a hamburger. How much change will he get back from $20.00?

10) _____ What is the total cost of a deluxe cheeseburger and a taco if there is a five percent sales tax?

Happy Turtle Press   Shopping Problems

J) Solve.

hot dog = $1.60	cola = $1.30
order of French-fries = $1.30	ice cream cone = $1.30
hamburger = $2.80	milk shake = $2.20
deluxe cheeseburger = $3.60	taco = $2.40

1) _____ What is the total cost of a deluxe cheeseburger and a hamburger if the sales tax is five percent?

2) _____ What is the total cost of an ice cream cone, a hot dog, and a milk shake if there is a five percent sales tax?

3) _____ If Allan wanted to buy a hot dog, how much money would he need?

4) _____ What is the total cost of an order of French-fries if there is a five percent sales tax?

5) _____ Marin wants to buy an order of French-fries. How much money will she need?

6) _____ If Jennifer wanted to buy a milk shake and a hot dog, how much would she have to pay?

7) _____ What is the total cost of a deluxe cheeseburger?

8) _____ What is the total cost of an ice cream cone, a milk shake, and an order of French-fries?

9) _____ Marcie purchases a deluxe cheeseburger. If she had $10.00, how much money will she have left?

10) _____ If Donald wanted to buy an ice cream cone, an order of French-fries, and a deluxe cheeseburger, how much money would he need?

K) Solve.

hot dog = $1.25	cola = $1.25
order of French-fries = $1.00	ice cream cone = $1.25
hamburger = $2.00	milk shake = $2.50
deluxe cheeseburger = $3.75	taco = $2.50

1) _____ Amy purchases a hamburger and a milk shake. If she had $10.00, how much money will she have left?

2) _____ If Sandra wanted to buy a hot dog and a hamburger, how much would it cost her?

3) _____ Michele purchases a cola. If she had $5.00, how much money will she have left?

4) _____ Marin wants to buy a deluxe cheeseburger. How much will she have to pay?

5) _____ Brian wants to buy a milk shake. How much will it cost him?

6) _____ If Allan buys a milk shake, how much money will he get back if he pays $5.00?

7) _____ Janet purchases a hamburger, a milk shake, and a cola. If she had $10.00, how much money will she have left?

8) _____ If Paul buys a hot dog, how much money will he get back if he pays $10.00?

9) _____ What is the total cost of an order of French-fries if the sales tax is 5%?

10) _____ If Marcie wanted to buy a milk shake, how much would it cost her?

L) Solve.

hot dog = $1.75	cola = $1.00
order of French-fries = $1.25	ice cream cone = $1.50
hamburger = $2.50	milk shake = $2.25
deluxe cheeseburger = $3.50	taco = $2.25

1) _____ If Brian buys a hot dog and a taco, and if he had $10.00, how much money will he have left?

2) _____ Janet purchases a deluxe cheeseburger, an order of French-fries, and an ice cream cone. If she had $10.00, how much money will she have left?

3) _____ Sharon wants to buy a cola. How much money will she need?

4) _____ What is the total cost of a hot dog and an order of French-fries?

5) _____ If Jackie buys an order of French-fries, what will her change be if she pays $10.00?

6) _____ Steven purchases a hamburger and a deluxe cheeseburger. If he had $10.00, how much money will he have left?

7) _____ What is the total cost of an ice cream cone and a milk shake if there is a 5% sales tax?

8) _____ If Marin buys a hamburger and a cola, and if she had $10.00, how much money will she have left?

9) _____ Billy wants to buy a milk shake, a deluxe cheeseburger, and a cola. How much money will he need?

10) _____ If Donald wanted to buy an order of French-fries, how much would he have to pay?

M) Solve.

hot dog = $1.25	cola = $1.25
order of French-fries = $1.00	ice cream cone = $1.75
hamburger = $2.25	milk shake = $2.50
deluxe cheeseburger = $3.75	taco = $2.25

1) _____ If Jackie wanted to buy a hot dog, how much would she have to pay?

2) _____ If Audrey wanted to buy an order of French-fries and a taco, how much money would she need?

3) _____ Paul purchases a hot dog. How much money will he get back if he pays $10.00?

4) _____ Ellen purchases an ice cream cone, a hot dog, and a milk shake. If she had $20.00, how much money will she have left?

5) _____ If Brian wanted to buy a hot dog and a deluxe cheeseburger, how much money would he need?

6) _____ Sharon wants to buy an order of French-fries. How much money will she need?

7) _____ What is the total cost of a hamburger and a milk shake?

8) _____ What is the total cost of a hot dog and a hamburger if the sales tax is 5%?

9) _____ Steven wants to buy an ice cream cone and a milk shake. How much will it cost him?

10) _____ If Sandra wanted to buy a hot dog, a taco, and a hamburger, how much would it cost her?

N) Solve.

hot dog = $2.00	cola = $1.25
order of French-fries = $0.75	ice cream cone = $1.25
hamburger = $2.25	milk shake = $2.00
deluxe cheeseburger = $3.25	taco = $2.50

1) _____ Allan purchases an order of French-fries, a milk shake, and an ice cream cone. How much change will he get back from $10.00?

2) _____ If Marin buys a hot dog, an order of French-fries, and an ice cream cone, and if she had $10.00, how much money will she have left?

3) _____ What is the total cost of a hot dog?

4) _____ What is the total cost of a hot dog, an order of French-fries, and a milk shake?

5) _____ If Sharon buys a hamburger, a deluxe cheeseburger, and a taco, and if she had $15.00, how much money will she have left?

6) _____ If Sandra buys a hot dog, and if she had $5.00, how much money will she have left?

7) _____ If Ellen wanted to buy an ice cream cone, a hot dog, and a deluxe cheeseburger, how much would she have to pay?

8) _____ What is the total cost of a milk shake if the sales tax is 5%?

9) _____ Amy wants to buy a hot dog, a milk shake, and a cola. How much will it cost her?

10) _____ What is the total cost of a taco and a hot dog if the sales tax is five percent?

O) Solve.

hot dog = $1.00	cola = $1.25
order of French-fries = $1.25	ice cream cone = $1.50
hamburger = $2.25	milk shake = $2.00
deluxe cheeseburger = $3.50	taco = $2.25

1) _____ What is the total cost of an ice cream cone?

2) _____ If Jennifer wanted to buy a cola, a deluxe cheeseburger, and a taco, how much would it cost her?

3) _____ What is the total cost of a hot dog, a taco, and a milk shake if the sales tax is 5%?

4) _____ If Amy buys a milk shake, how much change will she get back from $10.00?

5) _____ What is the total cost of a taco, an ice cream cone, and a cola?

6) _____ If David wanted to buy an order of French-fries, how much would he have to pay?

7) _____ What is the total cost of a cola, an ice cream cone, and a hot dog?

8) _____ If Donald buys a taco, what will his change be if he pays $10.00?

9) _____ Paul purchases a milk shake and an ice cream cone. If he had $10.00, how much money will he have left?

10) _____ What is the total cost of a milk shake and a taco?

P) Solve.

hot dog = $1.50	cola = $1.00
order of French-fries = $1.00	ice cream cone = $1.50
hamburger = $3.00	milk shake = $2.50
deluxe cheeseburger = $3.50	taco = $2.50

1) _____ What is the total cost of a hamburger if the sales tax is 5%?

2) _____ Ellen wants to buy a milk shake. How much will it cost her?

3) _____ If Steven wanted to buy an order of French-fries, how much money would he need?

4) _____ Marin wants to buy a milk shake, a cola, and a deluxe cheeseburger. How much will she have to pay?

5) _____ Jake purchases a deluxe cheeseburger. If he had $10.00, how much money will he have left?

6) _____ What is the total cost of an ice cream cone and a milk shake?

7) _____ If David wanted to buy a cola and an ice cream cone, how much would he have to pay?

8) _____ What is the total cost of an order of French-fries, a milk shake, and a deluxe cheeseburger?

9) _____ What is the total cost of a hot dog if the sales tax is five percent?

10) _____ If Jennifer buys a hot dog, how much change will she get back from $5.00?

Q) Solve.

hot dog = $1.50	cola = $1.00
order of French-fries = $0.50	ice cream cone = $1.00
hamburger = $2.00	milk shake = $2.50
deluxe cheeseburger = $3.00	taco = $2.50

1) _____ Adam wants to buy a milk shake and an ice cream cone. How much will it cost him?

2) _____ What is the total cost of a deluxe cheeseburger if there is a five percent sales tax?

3) _____ If Billy buys a milk shake, what will his change be if he pays $10.00?

4) _____ Ellen purchases a hamburger, a hot dog, and a taco. How much money will she get back if she pays $20.00?

5) _____ Marcie purchases a milk shake. If she had $10.00, how much money will she have left?

6) _____ Sandra purchases a deluxe cheeseburger and a cola. What will her change be if she pays $10.00?

7) _____ If Janet wanted to buy a hot dog, how much would it cost her?

8) _____ What is the total cost of a milk shake and a taco?

9) _____ If Jake wanted to buy a milk shake and a deluxe cheeseburger, how much money would he need?

10) _____ What is the total cost of an order of French-fries and a cola?

R) Solve.

hot dog = $1.00	cola = $1.00
order of French-fries = $0.50	ice cream cone = $1.00
hamburger = $2.50	milk shake = $2.50
deluxe cheeseburger = $3.50	taco = $2.50

1) _____ What is the total cost of a milk shake, a deluxe cheeseburger, and a hot dog?

2) _____ What is the total cost of a cola, a taco, and a hot dog?

3) _____ What is the total cost of a deluxe cheeseburger if the sales tax is 5%?

4) _____ Janet wants to buy an ice cream cone and an order of French-fries. How much will she have to pay?

5) _____ What is the total cost of a cola?

6) _____ Steven purchases an order of French-fries, an ice cream cone, and a milk shake. What will his change be if he pays $10.00?

7) _____ Marcie wants to buy a deluxe cheeseburger. How much will it cost her?

8) _____ What is the total cost of a hamburger if the sales tax is five percent?

9) _____ Sandra purchases a hot dog, a cola, and a milk shake. How much change will she get back from $10.00?

10) _____ What is the total cost of a milk shake and a deluxe cheeseburger if the sales tax is five percent?

S) Solve.

hot dog = $1.50	cola = $1.00
order of French-fries = $0.50	ice cream cone = $1.50
hamburger = $2.00	milk shake = $2.50
deluxe cheeseburger = $3.50	taco = $2.50

1) _____ What is the total cost of a cola?

2) _____ What is the total cost of an order of French-fries?

3) _____ Allan wants to buy an order of French-fries and a hamburger. How much will he have to pay?

4) _____ Janet purchases an order of French-fries. What will her change be if she pays $5.00?

5) _____ What is the total cost of an order of French-fries, a milk shake, and an ice cream cone if the sales tax is five percent?

6) _____ Ellen wants to buy a hot dog and an ice cream cone. How much will she have to pay?

7) _____ Brian purchases a taco. If he had $10.00, how much money will he have left?

8) _____ Sharon purchases a hot dog. How much change will she get back from $10.00?

9) _____ Jackie purchases a cola and a hamburger. If she had $10.00, how much money will she have left?

10) _____ What is the total cost of a hot dog and a cola?

T) Solve.

hot dog = $1.00	cola = $1.00
order of French-fries = $1.00	ice cream cone = $1.50
hamburger = $2.00	milk shake = $2.00
deluxe cheeseburger = $3.00	taco = $2.00

1) _____ Janet purchases a cola, a milk shake, and an order of French-fries. How much money will she get back if she pays $10.00?

2) _____ Audrey purchases a hamburger, an ice cream cone, and a hot dog. What will her change be if she pays $10.00?

3) _____ What is the total cost of an order of French-fries, a cola, and a hot dog if there is a 5% sales tax?

4) _____ What is the total cost of an order of French-fries?

5) _____ If Paul buys a hot dog, what will his change be if he pays $5.00?

6) _____ Jennifer wants to buy an order of French-fries. How much will she have to pay?

7) _____ What is the total cost of a milk shake?

8) _____ Steven wants to buy a hamburger and a cola. How much will it cost him?

9) _____ If Donald wanted to buy a deluxe cheeseburger, how much would he have to pay?

10) _____ If Jake buys a taco, and if he had $5.00, how much money will he have left?

U) Solve.

hot dog = $1.50	cola = $1.00
order of French-fries = $1.00	ice cream cone = $1.00
hamburger = $2.00	milk shake = $2.50
deluxe cheeseburger = $3.00	taco = $2.00

1) _____ If Steven buys an ice cream cone, a taco, and a hamburger, and if he had $10.00, how much money will he have left?

2) _____ What is the total cost of a milk shake, an ice cream cone, and an order of French-fries?

3) _____ If Sharon wanted to buy an order of French-fries and a deluxe cheeseburger, how much would it cost her?

4) _____ Brian wants to buy a hot dog. How much will it cost him?

5) _____ What is the total cost of a milk shake, a hot dog, and a hamburger?

6) _____ Marin wants to buy a cola. How much will it cost her?

7) _____ If Ellen wanted to buy an ice cream cone, how much would she have to pay?

8) _____ Allan purchases an order of French-fries. How much change will he get back from $5.00?

9) _____ If Jennifer wanted to buy a milk shake and a cola, how much would it cost her?

10) _____ Jackie wants to buy a deluxe cheeseburger, a milk shake, and a taco. How much money will she need?

V) Solve.

hot dog = $1.00	cola = $1.00
order of French-fries = $1.00	ice cream cone = $1.00
hamburger = $2.00	milk shake = $2.00
deluxe cheeseburger = $3.50	taco = $2.50

1) _____ What is the total cost of a taco and a hamburger if there is a 5% sales tax?

2) _____ If Jake buys a cola and an ice cream cone, how much money will he get back if he pays $10.00?

3) _____ If Audrey wanted to buy an ice cream cone and a taco, how much would she have to pay?

4) _____ Brian purchases a cola and a taco. What will his change be if he pays $10.00?

5) _____ If Donald wanted to buy a hot dog, how much would it cost him?

6) _____ What is the total cost of an order of French-fries and a deluxe cheeseburger?

7) _____ If Amy buys a hamburger, how much change will she get back from $5.00?

8) _____ What is the total cost of an ice cream cone if the sales tax is 5%?

9) _____ What is the total cost of a taco and a cola?

10) _____ What is the total cost of a milk shake, a hot dog, and an order of French-fries?

W) Solve.

hot dog = $1.00	cola = $1.00
order of French-fries = $1.00	ice cream cone = $1.50
hamburger = $2.50	milk shake = $2.00
deluxe cheeseburger = $3.50	taco = $2.50

1) _____ If Sharon wanted to buy a cola and an order of French-fries, how much would she have to pay?

2) _____ If David wanted to buy a hamburger, a hot dog, and a taco, how much would it cost him?

3) _____ If Donald wanted to buy a deluxe cheeseburger, a cola, and a milk shake, how much would he have to pay?

4) _____ What is the total cost of an ice cream cone?

5) _____ If Ellen wanted to buy a taco, a cola, and a milk shake, how much would she have to pay?

6) _____ Jackie purchases a hot dog, a taco, and an ice cream cone. If she had $10.00, how much money will she have left?

7) _____ What is the total cost of a cola, an order of French-fries, and a deluxe cheeseburger if there is a five percent sales tax?

8) _____ What is the total cost of a hamburger, a hot dog, and an ice cream cone?

9) _____ What is the total cost of a cola if the sales tax is 5%?

10) _____ If Sandra wanted to buy a hamburger, a deluxe cheeseburger, and a taco, how much money would she need?

Happy Turtle Press   Shopping Problems

X) Solve.

hot dog = $1.00	cola = $1.00
order of French-fries = $0.50	ice cream cone = $1.00
hamburger = $2.50	milk shake = $2.50
deluxe cheeseburger = $3.00	taco = $2.00

1) _____ Janet purchases an ice cream cone, a taco, and a cola. If she had $10.00, how much money will she have left?

2) _____ If Adam buys a cola, a taco, and a hot dog, how much money will he get back if he pays $10.00?

3) _____ What is the total cost of a hamburger, an ice cream cone, and a hot dog?

4) _____ Sharon purchases a cola, a hot dog, and an ice cream cone. How much change will she get back from $10.00?

5) _____ If Marcie buys a hot dog, a hamburger, and a taco, and if she had $20.00, how much money will she have left?

6) _____ Jackie wants to buy a milk shake, a hot dog, and a hamburger. How much will she have to pay?

7) _____ Steven purchases a cola, an order of French-fries, and a hot dog. How much change will he get back from $5.00?

8) _____ Sandra purchases an ice cream cone and a cola. How much money will she get back if she pays $10.00?

9) _____ What is the total cost of a hot dog and an ice cream cone if there is a 5% sales tax?

10) _____ What is the total cost of a milk shake?

Happy Turtle Press   Shopping Problems

Y) Solve.

hot dog = $1.50	cola = $1.00
order of French-fries = $1.00	ice cream cone = $1.50
hamburger = $2.00	milk shake = $2.50
deluxe cheeseburger = $3.00	taco = $2.50

1) _____ If Adam buys an order of French-fries and a hamburger, how much change will he get back from $10.00?

2) _____ Amy wants to buy a cola and a milk shake. How much money will she need?

3) _____ Jake wants to buy a cola and a deluxe cheeseburger. How much will he have to pay?

4) _____ If Steven buys a hamburger, how much change will he get back from $5.00?

5) _____ If Allan wanted to buy a taco, how much money would he need?

6) _____ Donald wants to buy a taco, a deluxe cheeseburger, and an ice cream cone. How much will he have to pay?

7) _____ If Janet buys a hamburger, an ice cream cone, and a taco, and if she had $10.00, how much money will she have left?

8) _____ If Ellen buys a taco, a milk shake, and an order of French-fries, what will her change be if she pays $20.00?

9) _____ What is the total cost of a deluxe cheeseburger if the sales tax is five percent?

10) _____ David wants to buy a hot dog. How much money will he need?

Z) Solve.

hot dog = $1.00	cola = $1.00
order of French-fries = $0.00	ice cream cone = $1.00
hamburger = $2.00	milk shake = $2.00
deluxe cheeseburger = $3.00	taco = $2.00

1) _____ Sharon purchases a deluxe cheeseburger. How much money will she get back if she pays $10.00?

2) _____ If Ellen wanted to buy an ice cream cone, a cola, and a deluxe cheeseburger, how much would it cost her?

3) _____ If Billy buys a deluxe cheeseburger and an order of French-fries, how much change will he get back from $10.00?

4) _____ What is the total cost of a milk shake if there is a 5% sales tax?

5) _____ If Marcie wanted to buy a taco, how much would she have to pay?

6) _____ Donald wants to buy a taco, a cola, and a hamburger. How much money will he need?

7) _____ If Jackie buys a milk shake and a taco, how much change will she get back from $10.00?

8) _____ Janet purchases a cola. How much change will she get back from $5.00?

9) _____ What is the total cost of an order of French-fries and a deluxe cheeseburger?

10) _____ What is the total cost of a hamburger?

AA) Solve.

hot dog = $1.00	cola = $1.00
order of French-fries = $1.00	ice cream cone = $1.00
hamburger = $2.00	milk shake = $2.00
deluxe cheeseburger = $3.00	taco = $2.00

1) _____ If Sandra buys a deluxe cheeseburger and an order of French-fries, what will her change be if she pays $10.00?

2) _____ Brian wants to buy a taco, an order of French-fries, and a hamburger. How much money will he need?

3) _____ If Jackie buys an order of French-fries, a taco, and a deluxe cheeseburger, how much change will she get back from $10.00?

4) _____ Amy purchases an ice cream cone. How much change will she get back from $10.00?

5) _____ Allan wants to buy a deluxe cheeseburger and a hot dog. How much will it cost him?

6) _____ What is the total cost of a cola and a taco if the sales tax is five percent?

7) _____ If Steven wanted to buy a taco and an order of French-fries, how much money would he need?

8) _____ What is the total cost of a hot dog?

9) _____ Ellen purchases a milk shake. What will her change be if she pays $10.00?

10) _____ What is the total cost of a milk shake and a deluxe cheeseburger if there is a 5% sales tax?

BB) Solve.

hot dog = $1.00	cola = $1.00
order of French-fries = $0.00	ice cream cone = $2.00
hamburger = $2.00	milk shake = $2.00
deluxe cheeseburger = $3.00	taco = $2.00

1) _____ What is the total cost of a hot dog, a taco, and a milk shake if the sales tax is 5%?

2) _____ If Janet buys a cola, how much change will she get back from $5.00?

3) _____ If Sharon buys a milk shake, a deluxe cheeseburger, and a hot dog, and if she had $20.00, how much money will she have left?

4) _____ Allan purchases an ice cream cone. How much money will he get back if he pays $5.00?

5) _____ Amy wants to buy a milk shake, a cola, and a hamburger. How much money will she need?

6) _____ If Steven buys a hamburger, how much money will he get back if he pays $5.00?

7) _____ Michele purchases a deluxe cheeseburger and a taco. What will her change be if she pays $10.00?

8) _____ If David buys a taco and a deluxe cheeseburger, what will his change be if he pays $10.00?

9) _____ What is the total cost of a taco?

10) _____ If Ellen wanted to buy a taco, a hamburger, and a hot dog, how much money would she need?

CC) Solve.

hot dog = $1.00	cola = $1.00
order of French-fries = $0.00	ice cream cone = $1.00
hamburger = $2.00	milk shake = $2.00
deluxe cheeseburger = $3.00	taco = $2.00

1) _____ What is the total cost of a hamburger?

2) _____ Paul purchases a hot dog. What will his change be if he pays $5.00?

3) _____ What is the total cost of a hot dog, a cola, and an ice cream cone if the sales tax is 5%?

4) _____ Sharon purchases a milk shake, a hamburger, and an order of French-fries. What will her change be if she pays $10.00?

5) _____ Audrey purchases a milk shake and a cola. What will her change be if she pays $10.00?

6) _____ Adam purchases a milk shake, a hamburger, and a hot dog. How much change will he get back from $10.00?

7) _____ If Steven wanted to buy a taco, a milk shake, and a hamburger, how much would he have to pay?

8) _____ If Amy buys an order of French-fries, how much money will she get back if she pays $5.00?

9) _____ What is the total cost of a taco and a hamburger if there is a 5% sales tax?

10) _____ If Michele buys a cola, a deluxe cheeseburger, and a hamburger, what will her change be if she pays $20.00?

DD) Solve.

hot dog = $1.00	cola = $1.00
order of French-fries = $0.00	ice cream cone = $1.00
hamburger = $2.00	milk shake = $2.00
deluxe cheeseburger = $3.00	taco = $2.00

1) _____ What is the total cost of an ice cream cone and a cola if the sales tax is 5%?

2) _____ What is the total cost of an ice cream cone, a cola, and a hot dog if the sales tax is 5%?

3) _____ If Michele wanted to buy a hot dog and a milk shake, how much money would she need?

4) _____ What is the total cost of an order of French-fries?

5) _____ What is the total cost of an ice cream cone and a deluxe cheeseburger?

6) _____ What is the total cost of a milk shake?

7) _____ What is the total cost of a taco, a milk shake, and an ice cream cone if there is a five percent sales tax?

8) _____ What is the total cost of a hot dog, a cola, and a taco if there is a five percent sales tax?

9) _____ If Ellen buys a cola and a taco, and if she had $10.00, how much money will she have left?

10) _____ If Marin buys an ice cream cone and a cola, how much change will she get back from $5.00?

EE) Solve.

hot dog = $1.00	cola = $1.00
order of French-fries = $1.00	ice cream cone = $1.00
hamburger = $2.00	milk shake = $2.00
deluxe cheeseburger = $3.00	taco = $2.00

1) _____ If Paul wanted to buy a milk shake, a deluxe cheeseburger, and a hamburger, how much money would he need?

2) _____ What is the total cost of a taco, a milk shake, and a cola?

3) _____ If Janet wanted to buy a hamburger and a taco, how much would it cost her?

4) _____ Jackie purchases a cola and a milk shake. How much change will she get back from $10.00?

5) _____ What is the total cost of a milk shake, a taco, and a hamburger if the sales tax is 5%?

6) _____ What is the total cost of a hamburger and a hot dog?

7) _____ Michele wants to buy a cola. How much will she have to pay?

8) _____ Jennifer purchases a hot dog, an ice cream cone, and a taco. How much money will she get back if she pays $10.00?

9) _____ What is the total cost of an order of French-fries?

10) _____ What is the total cost of a hamburger and a cola if there is a five percent sales tax?

FF) Solve.

hot dog = $1.00	cola = $1.00
order of French-fries = $0.00	ice cream cone = $1.00
hamburger = $2.00	milk shake = $2.00
deluxe cheeseburger = $3.00	taco = $2.00

1) _____ What is the total cost of a hot dog and a deluxe cheeseburger?

2) _____ What is the total cost of a hot dog, an order of French-fries, and a deluxe cheeseburger if there is a five percent sales tax?

3) _____ Sharon wants to buy an ice cream cone, a milk shake, and a deluxe cheeseburger. How much will it cost her?

4) _____ If Ellen wanted to buy a milk shake, an order of French-fries, and a deluxe cheeseburger, how much money would she need?

5) _____ What is the total cost of a hamburger if the sales tax is 5%?

6) _____ What is the total cost of a hot dog if there is a 5% sales tax?

7) _____ If Amy buys a milk shake and a hamburger, what will her change be if she pays $10.00?

8) _____ Marin purchases a milk shake and a cola. If she had $10.00, how much money will she have left?

9) _____ David purchases a hot dog, a cola, and an order of French-fries. How much change will he get back from $10.00?

10) _____ Adam wants to buy a hot dog, an order of French-fries, and a cola. How much will he have to pay?

Happy Turtle Press   Shopping Problems

GG) Solve.

hot dog = $2.00	cola = $1.00
order of French-fries = $1.00	ice cream cone = $1.00
hamburger = $2.00	milk shake = $2.00
deluxe cheeseburger = $3.00	taco = $2.00

1) _____ Donald purchases a milk shake and a hamburger. How much change will he get back from $10.00?

2) _____ What is the total cost of a hot dog and a taco?

3) _____ If Brian wanted to buy a deluxe cheeseburger, a taco, and a hamburger, how much money would he need?

4) _____ Jake wants to buy an order of French-fries. How much will it cost him?

5) _____ What is the total cost of an order of French-fries and a deluxe cheeseburger if the sales tax is 5%?

6) _____ If Allan wanted to buy a hamburger, how much money would he need?

7) _____ What is the total cost of a deluxe cheeseburger, an ice cream cone, and an order of French-fries?

8) _____ Marcie wants to buy a taco. How much will she have to pay?

9) _____ If Billy buys a cola, a hamburger, and a taco, how much change will he get back from $10.00?

10) _____ Steven purchases a cola. How much money will he get back if he pays $5.00?

HH) Solve.

hot dog = $1.00	cola = $1.00
order of French-fries = $0.00	ice cream cone = $1.00
hamburger = $2.00	milk shake = $2.00
deluxe cheeseburger = $3.00	taco = $2.00

1) _____ If Sharon buys an order of French-fries, how much money will she get back if she pays $5.00?

2) _____ Jackie purchases a milk shake and a hot dog. How much money will she get back if she pays $10.00?

3) _____ If Marcie wanted to buy a hamburger, a taco, and an ice cream cone, how much money would she need?

4) _____ Janet wants to buy a cola, a taco, and a milk shake. How much will she have to pay?

5) _____ Billy purchases an ice cream cone. If he had $10.00, how much money will he have left?

6) _____ If Amy buys a hamburger, a cola, and a hot dog, and if she had $10.00, how much money will she have left?

7) _____ If Adam buys a cola and a hot dog, how much money will he get back if he pays $5.00?

8) _____ What is the total cost of an ice cream cone and an order of French-fries if the sales tax is 5%?

9) _____ What is the total cost of an order of French-fries, an ice cream cone, and a milk shake if there is a five percent sales tax?

10) _____ Jake purchases a hamburger, a hot dog, and a cola. What will his change be if he pays $10.00?

II) Solve.

hot dog = $1.00	cola = $1.00
order of French-fries = $0.00	ice cream cone = $1.00
hamburger = $2.00	milk shake = $2.00
deluxe cheeseburger = $3.00	taco = $2.00

1) _____ What is the total cost of an ice cream cone, a hamburger, and a deluxe cheeseburger?

2) _____ What is the total cost of an ice cream cone?

3) _____ Donald wants to buy an order of French-fries and a deluxe cheeseburger. How much will he have to pay?

4) _____ What is the total cost of a hot dog, a deluxe cheeseburger, and a taco if the sales tax is five percent?

5) _____ Janet wants to buy a milk shake, an ice cream cone, and a hamburger. How much will she have to pay?

6) _____ If Ellen buys a taco, an ice cream cone, and a cola, and if she had $10.00, how much money will she have left?

7) _____ Michele purchases a hot dog and a hamburger. If she had $10.00, how much money will she have left?

8) _____ Jake purchases a hamburger and an order of French-fries. If he had $5.00, how much money will he have left?

9) _____ If Allan buys an ice cream cone and a hot dog, and if he had $10.00, how much money will he have left?

10) _____ If Paul wanted to buy a hamburger and a hot dog, how much money would he need?

JJ) Solve.

hot dog = $1.00	cola = $1.00
order of French-fries = $1.00	ice cream cone = $1.00
hamburger = $2.00	milk shake = $2.00
deluxe cheeseburger = $3.00	taco = $2.00

1) _____ What is the total cost of an order of French-fries?

2) _____ If Marcie buys a hot dog, a hamburger, and an ice cream cone, and if she had $10.00, how much money will she have left?

3) _____ If Audrey wanted to buy an order of French-fries, an ice cream cone, and a hamburger, how much would she have to pay?

4) _____ If Ellen buys a cola, how much money will she get back if she pays $10.00?

5) _____ What is the total cost of a deluxe cheeseburger?

6) _____ If Jackie buys a hamburger and a cola, what will her change be if she pays $10.00?

7) _____ Billy purchases a cola. What will his change be if he pays $5.00?

8) _____ Michele purchases a cola and a milk shake. What will her change be if she pays $10.00?

9) _____ What is the total cost of an order of French-fries, a cola, and an ice cream cone if the sales tax is 5%?

10) _____ What is the total cost of an ice cream cone if the sales tax is 5%?

KK) Solve.

hot dog = $1.00	cola = $1.00
order of French-fries = $0.00	ice cream cone = $1.00
hamburger = $2.00	milk shake = $2.00
deluxe cheeseburger = $3.00	taco = $2.00

1) _____ Marcie wants to buy a milk shake and a deluxe cheeseburger. How much will it cost her?

2) _____ What is the total cost of an order of French-fries, a cola, and a deluxe cheeseburger if the sales tax is five percent?

3) _____ Jake purchases a hot dog. How much change will he get back from $5.00?

4) _____ Adam wants to buy a milk shake. How much money will he need?

5) _____ What is the total cost of a hamburger?

6) _____ Jennifer purchases a hamburger, a deluxe cheeseburger, and a taco. How much money will she get back if she pays $20.00?

7) _____ If Steven buys a milk shake and a hamburger, and if he had $10.00, how much money will he have left?

8) _____ If Ellen wanted to buy a cola, an ice cream cone, and a hot dog, how much would it cost her?

9) _____ If Allan buys a hot dog, an ice cream cone, and a cola, what will his change be if he pays $10.00?

10) _____ If Brian buys an order of French-fries, what will his change be if he pays $5.00?

Happy Turtle Press • Shopping Problems

LL) Solve.

hot dog = $1.00	cola = $1.00
order of French-fries = $0.00	ice cream cone = $1.00
hamburger = $2.00	milk shake = $2.00
deluxe cheeseburger = $3.00	taco = $2.00

1) _____ If Brian buys a hamburger, how much change will he get back from $5.00?

2) _____ What is the total cost of a hamburger and a taco if there is a 5% sales tax?

3) _____ David purchases a deluxe cheeseburger. How much money will he get back if he pays $10.00?

4) _____ If Adam buys a hamburger, and if he had $10.00, how much money will he have left?

5) _____ If Marin wanted to buy a hot dog and a deluxe cheeseburger, how much would it cost her?

6) _____ What is the total cost of an ice cream cone and a hot dog?

7) _____ If Audrey wanted to buy a taco, an order of French-fries, and an ice cream cone, how much money would she need?

8) _____ Jennifer purchases a taco. How much money will she get back if she pays $10.00?

9) _____ If Sharon buys a hot dog, an order of French-fries, and a hamburger, what will her change be if she pays $10.00?

10) _____ What is the total cost of a hot dog if there is a 5% sales tax?

MM) Solve.

hot dog = $1.00	cola = $1.00
order of French-fries = $1.00	ice cream cone = $1.00
hamburger = $2.00	milk shake = $2.00
deluxe cheeseburger = $3.00	taco = $2.00

1) _____ Amy wants to buy an order of French-fries, an ice cream cone, and a milk shake. How much money will she need?

2) _____ If Jake wanted to buy a deluxe cheeseburger and a hamburger, how much would it cost him?

3) _____ Ellen purchases a hot dog and a hamburger. How much change will she get back from $10.00?

4) _____ What is the total cost of an ice cream cone?

5) _____ If Marcie buys an order of French-fries and a cola, what will her change be if she pays $10.00?

6) _____ If Adam buys an ice cream cone and a milk shake, how much money will he get back if he pays $10.00?

7) _____ If Jackie buys an order of French-fries, how much money will she get back if she pays $5.00?

8) _____ If Sharon wanted to buy a hot dog, a hamburger, and an ice cream cone, how much would it cost her?

9) _____ If Steven buys a cola and a deluxe cheeseburger, how much change will he get back from $10.00?

10) _____ What is the total cost of an ice cream cone, a hot dog, and an order of French-fries?

NN) Solve.

hot dog = $1.00	cola = $1.00
order of French-fries = $1.00	ice cream cone = $1.00
hamburger = $2.00	milk shake = $2.00
deluxe cheeseburger = $3.00	taco = $2.00

1) _____ If Sharon buys a deluxe cheeseburger, an order of French-fries, and a hamburger, how much money will she get back if she pays $20.00?

2) _____ What is the total cost of a milk shake and a hot dog?

3) _____ What is the total cost of an ice cream cone, a taco, and a deluxe cheeseburger if there is a fifteen percent sales tax?

4) _____ What is the total cost of a taco and a hamburger?

5) _____ Brian purchases an order of French-fries, an ice cream cone, and a cola. What will his change be if he pays $10.00?

6) _____ What is the total cost of a taco if the sales tax is 15%?

7) _____ If David wanted to buy an order of French-fries, how much would it cost him?

8) _____ What is the total cost of a hot dog, an order of French-fries, and a taco if the sales tax is 15%?

9) _____ Allan wants to buy a deluxe cheeseburger. How much money will he need?

10) _____ If Steven wanted to buy a taco, how much would he have to pay?

OO) Solve.

hot dog = $1.00	cola = $1.00
order of French-fries = $1.00	ice cream cone = $1.00
hamburger = $2.00	milk shake = $2.00
deluxe cheeseburger = $3.00	taco = $2.00

1) _____ What is the total cost of a milk shake?

2) _____ Marin purchases a milk shake. What will her change be if she pays $10.00?

3) _____ Sandra wants to buy a cola and an order of French-fries. How much will she have to pay?

4) _____ Allan purchases a milk shake, a deluxe cheeseburger, and a hamburger. What will his change be if he pays $10.00?

5) _____ What is the total cost of a hot dog and a milk shake?

6) _____ Michele purchases a taco, a cola, and a hamburger. If she had $10.00, how much money will she have left?

7) _____ What is the total cost of a cola, an ice cream cone, and a hamburger?

8) _____ If Sharon buys a milk shake, and if she had $5.00, how much money will she have left?

9) _____ Jennifer purchases an order of French-fries and a taco. What will her change be if she pays $10.00?

10) _____ If Steven wanted to buy a cola and a hot dog, how much would it cost him?

PP) Solve.

hot dog = $1.00	cola = $1.00
order of French-fries = $0.00	ice cream cone = $1.00
hamburger = $2.00	milk shake = $2.00
deluxe cheeseburger = $3.00	taco = $2.00

1) _____ If Marcie wanted to buy a cola, how much would she have to pay?

2) _____ What is the total cost of a milk shake, a hot dog, and an order of French-fries if there is a 15% sales tax?

3) _____ What is the total cost of a hamburger and a deluxe cheeseburger?

4) _____ If Ellen buys a deluxe cheeseburger, a milk shake, and a hot dog, how much change will she get back from $20.00?

5) _____ What is the total cost of a milk shake and an order of French-fries if there is a 15% sales tax?

6) _____ Paul wants to buy an ice cream cone, a cola, and an order of French-fries. How much money will he need?

7) _____ Allan purchases a hot dog and a cola. How much money will he get back if he pays $5.00?

8) _____ What is the total cost of an order of French-fries and a taco?

9) _____ What is the total cost of a deluxe cheeseburger?

10) _____ What is the total cost of a hot dog if there is a 15% sales tax?

QQ) Solve.

hot dog = $1.00	cola = $1.00
order of French-fries = $1.00	ice cream cone = $1.00
hamburger = $2.00	milk shake = $2.00
deluxe cheeseburger = $3.00	taco = $2.00

1) _____ If Audrey wanted to buy a hamburger and an ice cream cone, how much would it cost her?

2) _____ What is the total cost of a hamburger, a cola, and a hot dog if the sales tax is fifteen percent?

3) _____ Amy wants to buy an order of French-fries and an ice cream cone. How much money will she need?

4) _____ What is the total cost of a hot dog?

5) _____ Marcie purchases an order of French-fries and a deluxe cheeseburger. How much money will she get back if she pays $10.00?

6) _____ If Allan buys an ice cream cone and a milk shake, how much money will he get back if he pays $10.00?

7) _____ If Marin wanted to buy a hot dog, how much would it cost her?

8) _____ What is the total cost of a deluxe cheeseburger if there is a 15% sales tax?

9) _____ Janet purchases a milk shake. How much change will she get back from $5.00?

10) _____ What is the total cost of an order of French-fries and a deluxe cheeseburger?

Happy Turtle Press — Shopping Problems

RR) Solve.

hot dog = $1.00	cola = $1.00
order of French-fries = $1.00	ice cream cone = $1.00
hamburger = $2.00	milk shake = $2.00
deluxe cheeseburger = $3.00	taco = $2.00

1) _____ What is the total cost of a deluxe cheeseburger, an order of French-fries, and a taco?

2) _____ What is the total cost of a hot dog, a cola, and a deluxe cheeseburger?

3) _____ What is the total cost of a hamburger?

4) _____ Jackie purchases a hot dog. How much change will she get back from $5.00?

5) _____ Jennifer wants to buy a hamburger and a deluxe cheeseburger. How much will it cost her?

6) _____ If Steven buys a hot dog and an ice cream cone, what will his change be if he pays $5.00?

7) _____ If Marin wanted to buy a hot dog, how much money would she need?

8) _____ What is the total cost of a taco, an ice cream cone, and a hot dog?

9) _____ If Allan wanted to buy a hamburger and an ice cream cone, how much would he have to pay?

10) _____ If Janet buys a taco and a milk shake, and if she had $10.00, how much money will she have left?

SS) Solve.

hot dog = $1.00	cola = $1.00
order of French-fries = $1.00	ice cream cone = $1.00
hamburger = $2.00	milk shake = $2.00
deluxe cheeseburger = $3.00	taco = $2.00

1) _____ If Sandra buys a hot dog and a milk shake, how much change will she get back from $10.00?

2) _____ Audrey purchases a hot dog. How much money will she get back if she pays $5.00?

3) _____ What is the total cost of an order of French-fries, a hamburger, and a cola?

4) _____ What is the total cost of a deluxe cheeseburger and a taco if the sales tax is fifteen percent?

5) _____ What is the total cost of an order of French-fries?

6) _____ Marin wants to buy a taco and a milk shake. How much will she have to pay?

7) _____ Allan wants to buy a hamburger, a deluxe cheeseburger, and an ice cream cone. How much will it cost him?

8) _____ If Sharon wanted to buy a taco and an ice cream cone, how much money would she need?

9) _____ If Brian buys a milk shake, a hamburger, and an order of French-fries, and if he had $10.00, how much money will he have left?

10) _____ If Paul wanted to buy a hot dog, how much would it cost him?

TT) Solve.

hot dog = $1.00	cola = $1.00
order of French-fries = $0.00	ice cream cone = $1.00
hamburger = $2.00	milk shake = $2.00
deluxe cheeseburger = $3.00	taco = $2.00

1) _____ What is the total cost of four hot dogs and five ice cream cones?

2) _____ What is the total cost of five orders of French-fries, a milk shake, and a hot dog if there is a 15% sales tax?

3) _____ Michele purchases three ice cream cones. What will her change be if she pays $10.00?

4) _____ What is the total cost of an ice cream cone if there is a 15% sales tax?

5) _____ What is the total cost of a hamburger and three milk shakes?

6) _____ If Jackie wanted to buy five hamburgers, how much money would she need?

7) _____ What is the total cost of four ice cream cones?

8) _____ If Adam buys four milk shakes, what will his change be if he pays $15.00?

9) _____ If Sharon wanted to buy five milk shakes, three hamburgers, and two hot dogs, how much would she have to pay?

10) _____ If Steven wanted to buy two deluxe cheeseburgers, four ice cream cones, and three hot dogs, how much money would he need?

Happy Turtle Press   Shopping Problems

UU) Solve.

hot dog = $1.00	cola = $1.00
order of French-fries = $1.00	ice cream cone = $1.00
hamburger = $2.00	milk shake = $2.00
deluxe cheeseburger = $3.00	taco = $2.00

1) _____ What is the total cost of three orders of French-fries and five tacos?

2) _____ Michele purchases five colas. If she had $10.00, how much money will she have left?

3) _____ What is the total cost of five hamburgers and four deluxe cheeseburgers?

4) _____ What is the total cost of three hot dogs, three hamburgers, and four tacos if there is a 15% sales tax?

5) _____ What is the total cost of three tacos if there is a 15% sales tax?

6) _____ If Amy buys a milk shake, what will her change be if she pays $10.00?

7) _____ If Jake buys a hamburger and two ice cream cones, what will his change be if he pays $10.00?

8) _____ What is the total cost of two ice cream cones if the sales tax is fifteen percent?

9) _____ What is the total cost of five hamburgers if the sales tax is fifteen percent?

10) _____ David wants to buy an ice cream cone, four tacos, and a cola. How much money will he need?

Happy Turtle Press — Shopping Problems

VV) Solve.

hot dog = $1.00	cola = $1.00
order of French-fries = $1.00	ice cream cone = $1.00
hamburger = $2.00	milk shake = $2.00
deluxe cheeseburger = $3.00	taco = $2.00

1) _____ Allan wants to buy four hot dogs, five hamburgers, and two deluxe cheeseburgers. How much money will he need?

2) _____ What is the total cost of five deluxe cheeseburgers and four colas if the sales tax is fifteen percent?

3) _____ What is the total cost of three hamburgers?

4) _____ If Sandra wanted to buy three orders of French-fries and a milk shake, how much money would she need?

5) _____ If Audrey wanted to buy a taco, how much money would she need?

6) _____ What is the total cost of a cola?

7) _____ What is the total cost of two ice cream cones?

8) _____ Janet wants to buy four ice cream cones. How much will she have to pay?

9) _____ Ellen purchases a taco. If she had $10.00, how much money will she have left?

10) _____ If Paul wanted to buy five deluxe cheeseburgers, two tacos, and two colas, how much would he have to pay?

WW) Solve.

hot dog = $1.00	cola = $1.00
order of French-fries = $1.00	ice cream cone = $1.00
hamburger = $2.00	milk shake = $2.00
deluxe cheeseburger = $3.00	taco = $2.00

1) _____ What is the total cost of five hot dogs, three colas, and four tacos?

2) _____ Marcie purchases two orders of French-fries, four ice cream cones, and three deluxe cheeseburgers. How much money will she get back if she pays $30.00?

3) _____ Jake purchases four colas and five milk shakes. How much change will he get back from $20.00?

4) _____ Allan wants to buy three ice cream cones, three hamburgers, and three tacos. How much money will he need?

5) _____ What is the total cost of two milk shakes if the sales tax is 15%?

6) _____ If Billy wanted to buy two ice cream cones and five milk shakes, how much would it cost him?

7) _____ Sandra purchases a cola. If she had $10.00, how much money will she have left?

8) _____ What is the total cost of four orders of French-fries, three hot dogs, and three hamburgers if the sales tax is 15%?

9) _____ If Janet wanted to buy three hamburgers, three orders of French-fries, and three deluxe cheeseburgers, how much money would she need?

10) _____ Jennifer purchases five milk shakes, two hot dogs, and two hamburgers. How much change will she get back from $30.00?

XX) Solve.

hot dog = $1.00	cola = $1.00
order of French-fries = $1.00	ice cream cone = $1.00
hamburger = $2.00	milk shake = $2.00
deluxe cheeseburger = $3.00	taco = $2.00

1) _____ Audrey purchases five hot dogs. If she had $10.00, how much money will she have left?

2) _____ What is the total cost of five deluxe cheeseburgers, four ice cream cones, and three colas if the sales tax is fifteen percent?

3) _____ What is the total cost of three milk shakes if the sales tax is fifteen percent?

4) _____ What is the total cost of a deluxe cheeseburger, three milk shakes, and three hot dogs if there is a fifteen percent sales tax?

5) _____ If Steven wanted to buy a hamburger, how much would it cost him?

6) _____ Allan purchases three milk shakes, two tacos, and two ice cream cones. How much change will he get back from $15.00?

7) _____ If Michele buys two hamburgers, and if she had $10.00, how much money will she have left?

8) _____ Jennifer purchases three tacos, five orders of French-fries, and four hot dogs. If she had $30.00, how much money will she have left?

9) _____ Jake purchases two deluxe cheeseburgers, five milk shakes, and three hot dogs. If he had $30.00, how much money will he have left?

10) _____ Amy wants to buy a hot dog. How much will she have to pay?

A) Solve.

hot dog = $1.20	cola = $1.30
order of French-fries = $1.20	ice cream cone = $1.40
hamburger = $2.10	milk shake = $2.10
deluxe cheeseburger = $3.00	taco = $2.60

1) __$6.80__ Jackie wants to buy a deluxe cheeseburger, a hot dog, and a taco. How much will it cost her?

2) __$2.10__ Steven wants to buy a hamburger. How much will he have to pay?

3) __$14.30__ If Sandra buys a deluxe cheeseburger, an ice cream cone, and a cola, and if she had $20.00, how much money will she have left?

4) __$14.60__ Adam purchases a hamburger, a milk shake, and an order of French-fries. How much money will he get back if he pays $20.00?

5) __$5.30__ If Jake buys an ice cream cone, a hamburger, and a hot dog, what will his change be if he pays $10.00?

6) __$3.57__ What is the total cost of a cola and a hamburger if the sales tax is 5%?

7) __$12.30__ If Allan buys a taco, a deluxe cheeseburger, and a hamburger, how much change will he get back from $20.00?

8) __$8.60__ Brian purchases an ice cream cone. How much change will he get back from $10.00?

9) __$7.40__ If Ellen buys a taco, and if she had $10.00, how much money will she have left?

10) __$6.10__ Michele purchases a cola and a taco. How much change will she get back from $10.00?

B) Solve.

hot dog = $1.00	cola = $1.40
order of French-fries = $0.80	ice cream cone = $1.20
hamburger = $2.60	milk shake = $2.10
deluxe cheeseburger = $3.30	taco = $2.50

1) __$8.40__ What is the total cost of a deluxe cheeseburger, a milk shake, and a hamburger if there is a five percent sales tax?

2) __$8.60__ If David buys a cola, how much change will he get back from $10.00?

3) __$4.10__ What is the total cost of a cola and a taco if there is a five percent sales tax?

4) __$6.40__ What is the total cost of a milk shake, a hamburger, and a cola if there is a 5% sales tax?

5) __$4.70__ What is the total cost of a milk shake, an ice cream cone, and a cola?

6) __$4.94__ What is the total cost of a cola and a deluxe cheeseburger if there is a five percent sales tax?

7) __$5.50__ Jake wants to buy a milk shake, an order of French-fries, and a hamburger. How much will he have to pay?

8) __$2.60__ If Steven wanted to buy an ice cream cone and a cola, how much would it cost him?

9) __$4.10__ What is the total cost of an order of French-fries, a milk shake, and an ice cream cone?

10) __$2.90__ If Ellen buys a milk shake, and if she had $5.00, how much money will she have left?

C) Solve.

hot dog = $1.60	cola = $1.20
order of French-fries = $0.90	ice cream cone = $1.00
hamburger = $2.60	milk shake = $2.80
deluxe cheeseburger = $3.50	taco = $2.10

1) $0.90 If Jackie wanted to buy an order of French-fries, how much money would she need?

2) $4.90 What is the total cost of a milk shake and a taco?

3) $1.90 If Sharon wanted to buy an ice cream cone and an order of French-fries, how much would she have to pay?

4) $3.50 Donald purchases a taco, a milk shake, and a hot dog. How much money will he get back if he pays $10.00?

5) $4.90 If Jake wanted to buy an order of French-fries, a cola, and a milk shake, how much money would he need?

6) $4.30 If Marin wanted to buy an ice cream cone, a taco, and a cola, how much would she have to pay?

7) $6.80 If Michele wanted to buy a cola, a deluxe cheeseburger, and a taco, how much would it cost her?

8) $5.80 Sandra purchases an order of French-fries, a cola, and a taco. How much money will she get back if she pays $10.00?

9) $7.80 Jennifer purchases a cola and an ice cream cone. If she had $10.00, how much money will she have left?

10) $2.50 What is the total cost of a hot dog and an order of French-fries?

D) Solve.

hot dog = $1.60	cola = $1.10
order of French-fries = $0.70	ice cream cone = $1.90
hamburger = $2.80	milk shake = $2.00
deluxe cheeseburger = $3.70	taco = $2.90

1) $1.60   Sandra wants to buy a hot dog. How much will it cost her?

2) $5.20   Jackie purchases a cola and a deluxe cheeseburger. How much change will she get back from $10.00?

3) $14.10   David purchases a cola, an ice cream cone, and a taco. If he had $20.00, how much money will he have left?

4) $1.68   What is the total cost of a hot dog if there is a five percent sales tax?

5) $5.98   What is the total cost of a hamburger and a taco if the sales tax is five percent?

6) $3.10   If Donald wanted to buy a cola and a milk shake, how much would he have to pay?

7) $8.92   What is the total cost of a deluxe cheeseburger, a taco, and an ice cream cone if the sales tax is five percent?

8) $1.80   Billy wants to buy an order of French-fries and a cola. How much money will he need?

9) $7.10   Marin purchases a taco. How much change will she get back from $10.00?

10) $4.70   If Paul wanted to buy a cola, an order of French-fries, and a taco, how much would he have to pay?

E) Solve.

hot dog = $1.30	cola = $1.30
order of French-fries = $0.80	ice cream cone = $1.90
hamburger = $2.00	milk shake = $2.50
deluxe cheeseburger = $3.90	taco = $2.40

1) $14.80   If Audrey buys a hamburger, an ice cream cone, and a cola, and if she had $20.00, how much money will she have left?

2) $11.60   Michele purchases a deluxe cheeseburger, a hamburger, and a milk shake. How much change will she get back from $20.00?

3) $3.70   Adam wants to buy a cola and a taco. How much money will he need?

4) $2.00   If Ellen wanted to buy a hamburger, how much money would she need?

5) $1.90   Jennifer wants to buy an ice cream cone. How much money will she need?

6) $5.20   What is the total cost of a milk shake, an ice cream cone, and an order of French-fries?

7) $5.20   If Sharon wanted to buy a deluxe cheeseburger and a hot dog, how much money would she need?

8) $6.20   Jackie purchases a milk shake and a hot dog. If she had $10.00, how much money will she have left?

9) $6.80   Allan purchases an order of French-fries and a taco. How much money will he get back if he pays $10.00?

10) $8.08   What is the total cost of a deluxe cheeseburger, a hot dog, and a milk shake if the sales tax is 5%?

F) Solve.

hot dog = $1.40	cola = $1.10
order of French-fries = $0.80	ice cream cone = $1.20
hamburger = $2.80	milk shake = $2.00
deluxe cheeseburger = $3.60	taco = $2.40

1) $4.30   Sandra wants to buy a cola, a milk shake, and an ice cream cone. How much money will she need?

2) $5.80   Allan wants to buy a hot dog, a milk shake, and a taco. How much money will he need?

3) $6.10   Audrey purchases a hamburger and a cola. What will her change be if she pays $10.00?

4) $2.00   What is the total cost of a cola and an order of French-fries if the sales tax is 5%?

5) $3.78   What is the total cost of a taco and an ice cream cone if there is a five percent sales tax?

6) $3.20   If Jake wanted to buy an ice cream cone and a milk shake, how much would it cost him?

7) $5.60   Jennifer purchases a deluxe cheeseburger and an order of French-fries. How much change will she get back from $10.00?

8) $5.20   Donald wants to buy a taco and a hamburger. How much will it cost him?

9) $3.90   Janet purchases a cola. What will her change be if she pays $5.00?

10) $4.20   If Ellen buys a hot dog, a taco, and a milk shake, and if she had $10.00, how much money will she have left?

G) Solve.

hot dog = $1.00	cola = $1.10
order of French-fries = $1.30	ice cream cone = $1.10
hamburger = $2.10	milk shake = $2.10
deluxe cheeseburger = $3.90	taco = $2.20

1) $1.10   What is the total cost of an ice cream cone?

2) $13.90 If Donald buys a taco and a deluxe cheeseburger, and if he had $20.00, how much money will he have left?

3) $3.20   If Michele wanted to buy a hamburger and an ice cream cone, how much money would she need?

4) $2.90   If Marcie buys a hamburger, an ice cream cone, and a deluxe cheeseburger, how much money will she get back if she pays $10.00?

5) $1.05   What is the total cost of a hot dog if there is a 5% sales tax?

6) $3.20   What is the total cost of an ice cream cone and a milk shake?

7) $2.20   What is the total cost of a cola and a hot dog if there is a 5% sales tax?

8) $4.00   Audrey purchases a hot dog. If she had $5.00, how much money will she have left?

9) $2.80   Janet purchases a taco. How much money will she get back if she pays $5.00?

10) $4.72 What is the total cost of an ice cream cone, an order of French-fries, and a hamburger if the sales tax is 5%?

H) Solve.

hot dog = $1.00	cola = $1.00
order of French-fries = $0.80	ice cream cone = $1.10
hamburger = $2.90	milk shake = $2.20
deluxe cheeseburger = $3.70	taco = $3.00

1) $4.00   What is the total cost of a milk shake, an order of French-fries, and a hot dog?

2) $5.90   Jennifer wants to buy a milk shake and a deluxe cheeseburger. How much money will she need?

3) $3.70   If Paul wanted to buy a deluxe cheeseburger, how much money would he need?

4) $6.30   If Ellen buys an order of French-fries and a hamburger, how much change will she get back from $10.00?

5) $9.20   If Jackie buys an order of French-fries, how much change will she get back from $10.00?

6) $5.20   Amy purchases an order of French-fries, a taco, and a hot dog. If she had $10.00, how much money will she have left?

7) $1.90   Billy wants to buy an ice cream cone and an order of French-fries. How much money will he need?

8) $5.10   Allan wants to buy a milk shake and a hamburger. How much will it cost him?

9) $2.20   If David wanted to buy a milk shake, how much would it cost him?

10) $0.80   If Marcie wanted to buy an order of French-fries, how much would she have to pay?

I) Solve.

hot dog = $1.30	cola = $1.30
order of French-fries = $1.20	ice cream cone = $1.60
hamburger = $2.20	milk shake = $2.10
deluxe cheeseburger = $3.00	taco = $2.00

1) $2.20   Jackie wants to buy a hamburger. How much will it cost her?

2) $3.80   If Amy wanted to buy an ice cream cone and a hamburger, how much would it cost her?

3) $3.80   Michele wants to buy a cola, a hot dog, and an order of French-fries. How much will she have to pay?

4) $6.70   If Ellen buys a taco and a cola, and if she had $10.00, how much money will she have left?

5) $5.90   If Marin wanted to buy an ice cream cone, a deluxe cheeseburger, and a cola, how much would she have to pay?

6) $5.10   What is the total cost of a deluxe cheeseburger and a milk shake?

7) $4.20   If Billy wanted to buy a taco and a hamburger, how much money would he need?

8) $5.40   Sandra wants to buy a hot dog, a milk shake, and a taco. How much money will she need?

9) $14.50 Jake purchases a hot dog, a taco, and a hamburger. How much change will he get back from $20.00?

10) $5.25 What is the total cost of a deluxe cheeseburger and a taco if there is a five percent sales tax?

J) Solve.

hot dog = $1.60	cola = $1.30
order of French-fries = $1.30	ice cream cone = $1.30
hamburger = $2.80	milk shake = $2.20
deluxe cheeseburger = $3.60	taco = $2.40

1) $6.72   What is the total cost of a deluxe cheeseburger and a hamburger if the sales tax is five percent?

2) $5.36   What is the total cost of an ice cream cone, a hot dog, and a milk shake if there is a five percent sales tax?

3) $1.60   If Allan wanted to buy a hot dog, how much money would he need?

4) $1.36   What is the total cost of an order of French-fries if there is a five percent sales tax?

5) $1.30   Marin wants to buy an order of French-fries. How much money will she need?

6) $3.80   If Jennifer wanted to buy a milk shake and a hot dog, how much would she have to pay?

7) $3.60   What is the total cost of a deluxe cheeseburger?

8) $4.80   What is the total cost of an ice cream cone, a milk shake, and an order of French-fries?

9) $6.40   Marcie purchases a deluxe cheeseburger. If she had $10.00, how much money will she have left?

10) $6.20   If Donald wanted to buy an ice cream cone, an order of French-fries, and a deluxe cheeseburger, how much money would he need?

K) Solve.

hot dog = $1.25	cola = $1.25
order of French-fries = $1.00	ice cream cone = $1.25
hamburger = $2.00	milk shake = $2.50
deluxe cheeseburger = $3.75	taco = $2.50

1) $5.50   Amy purchases a hamburger and a milk shake. If she had $10.00, how much money will she have left?

2) $3.25   If Sandra wanted to buy a hot dog and a hamburger, how much would it cost her?

3) $3.75   Michele purchases a cola. If she had $5.00, how much money will she have left?

4) $3.75   Marin wants to buy a deluxe cheeseburger. How much will she have to pay?

5) $2.50   Brian wants to buy a milk shake. How much will it cost him?

6) $2.50   If Allan buys a milk shake, how much money will he get back if he pays $5.00?

7) $4.25   Janet purchases a hamburger, a milk shake, and a cola. If she had $10.00, how much money will she have left?

8) $8.75   If Paul buys a hot dog, how much money will he get back if he pays $10.00?

9) $1.05   What is the total cost of an order of French-fries if the sales tax is 5%?

10) $2.50   If Marcie wanted to buy a milk shake, how much would it cost her?

L) Solve.

hot dog = $1.75	cola = $1.00
order of French-fries = $1.25	ice cream cone = $1.50
hamburger = $2.50	milk shake = $2.25
deluxe cheeseburger = $3.50	taco = $2.25

1) $6.00   If Brian buys a hot dog and a taco, and if he had $10.00, how much money will he have left?

2) $3.75   Janet purchases a deluxe cheeseburger, an order of French-fries, and an ice cream cone. If she had $10.00, how much money will she have left?

3) $1.00   Sharon wants to buy a cola. How much money will she need?

4) $3.00   What is the total cost of a hot dog and an order of French-fries?

5) $8.75   If Jackie buys an order of French-fries, what will her change be if she pays $10.00?

6) $4.00   Steven purchases a hamburger and a deluxe cheeseburger. If he had $10.00, how much money will he have left?

7) $3.94   What is the total cost of an ice cream cone and a milk shake if there is a 5% sales tax?

8) $6.50   If Marin buys a hamburger and a cola, and if she had $10.00, how much money will she have left?

9) $6.75   Billy wants to buy a milk shake, a deluxe cheeseburger, and a cola. How much money will he need?

10) $1.25   If Donald wanted to buy an order of French-fries, how much would he have to pay?

M) Solve.

hot dog = $1.25	cola = $1.25
order of French-fries = $1.00	ice cream cone = $1.75
hamburger = $2.25	milk shake = $2.50
deluxe cheeseburger = $3.75	taco = $2.25

1) $1.25   If Jackie wanted to buy a hot dog, how much would she have to pay?

2) $3.25   If Audrey wanted to buy an order of French-fries and a taco, how much money would she need?

3) $8.75   Paul purchases a hot dog. How much money will he get back if he pays $10.00?

4) $14.50 Ellen purchases an ice cream cone, a hot dog, and a milk shake. If she had $20.00, how much money will she have left?

5) $5.00   If Brian wanted to buy a hot dog and a deluxe cheeseburger, how much money would he need?

6) $1.00   Sharon wants to buy an order of French-fries. How much money will she need?

7) $4.75   What is the total cost of a hamburger and a milk shake?

8) $3.68   What is the total cost of a hot dog and a hamburger if the sales tax is 5%?

9) $4.25   Steven wants to buy an ice cream cone and a milk shake. How much will it cost him?

10) $5.75 If Sandra wanted to buy a hot dog, a taco, and a hamburger, how much would it cost her?

N) Solve.

hot dog = $2.00	cola = $1.25
order of French-fries = $0.75	ice cream cone = $1.25
hamburger = $2.25	milk shake = $2.00
deluxe cheeseburger = $3.25	taco = $2.50

1) $6.00 Allan purchases an order of French-fries, a milk shake, and an ice cream cone. How much change will he get back from $10.00?

2) $6.00 If Marin buys a hot dog, an order of French-fries, and an ice cream cone, and if she had $10.00, how much money will she have left?

3) $2.00 What is the total cost of a hot dog?

4) $4.75 What is the total cost of a hot dog, an order of French-fries, and a milk shake?

5) $7.00 If Sharon buys a hamburger, a deluxe cheeseburger, and a taco, and if she had $15.00, how much money will she have left?

6) $3.00 If Sandra buys a hot dog, and if she had $5.00, how much money will she have left?

7) $6.50 If Ellen wanted to buy an ice cream cone, a hot dog, and a deluxe cheeseburger, how much would she have to pay?

8) $2.10 What is the total cost of a milk shake if the sales tax is 5%?

9) $5.25 Amy wants to buy a hot dog, a milk shake, and a cola. How much will it cost her?

10) $4.72 What is the total cost of a taco and a hot dog if the sales tax is five percent?

O) Solve.

hot dog = $1.00	cola = $1.25
order of French-fries = $1.25	ice cream cone = $1.50
hamburger = $2.25	milk shake = $2.00
deluxe cheeseburger = $3.50	taco = $2.25

1) $1.50   What is the total cost of an ice cream cone?

2) $7.00   If Jennifer wanted to buy a cola, a deluxe cheeseburger, and a taco, how much would it cost her?

3) $5.51   What is the total cost of a hot dog, a taco, and a milk shake if the sales tax is 5%?

4) $8.00   If Amy buys a milk shake, how much change will she get back from $10.00?

5) $5.00   What is the total cost of a taco, an ice cream cone, and a cola?

6) $1.25   If David wanted to buy an order of French-fries, how much would he have to pay?

7) $3.75   What is the total cost of a cola, an ice cream cone, and a hot dog?

8) $7.75   If Donald buys a taco, what will his change be if he pays $10.00?

9) $6.50   Paul purchases a milk shake and an ice cream cone. If he had $10.00, how much money will he have left?

10) $4.25   What is the total cost of a milk shake and a taco?

P) Solve.

hot dog = $1.50	cola = $1.00
order of French-fries = $1.00	ice cream cone = $1.50
hamburger = $3.00	milk shake = $2.50
deluxe cheeseburger = $3.50	taco = $2.50

1) $3.15   What is the total cost of a hamburger if the sales tax is 5%?

2) $2.50   Ellen wants to buy a milk shake. How much will it cost her?

3) $1.00   If Steven wanted to buy an order of French-fries, how much money would he need?

4) $7.00   Marin wants to buy a milk shake, a cola, and a deluxe cheeseburger. How much will she have to pay?

5) $6.50   Jake purchases a deluxe cheeseburger. If he had $10.00, how much money will he have left?

6) $4.00   What is the total cost of an ice cream cone and a milk shake?

7) $2.50   If David wanted to buy a cola and an ice cream cone, how much would he have to pay?

8) $7.00   What is the total cost of an order of French-fries, a milk shake, and a deluxe cheeseburger?

9) $1.58   What is the total cost of a hot dog if the sales tax is five percent?

10) $3.50   If Jennifer buys a hot dog, how much change will she get back from $5.00?

Q) Solve.

hot dog = $1.50	cola = $1.00
order of French-fries = $0.50	ice cream cone = $1.00
hamburger = $2.00	milk shake = $2.50
deluxe cheeseburger = $3.00	taco = $2.50

1) $3.50   Adam wants to buy a milk shake and an ice cream cone. How much will it cost him?

2) $3.15   What is the total cost of a deluxe cheeseburger if there is a five percent sales tax?

3) $7.50   If Billy buys a milk shake, what will his change be if he pays $10.00?

4) $14.00 Ellen purchases a hamburger, a hot dog, and a taco. How much money will she get back if she pays $20.00?

5) $7.50   Marcie purchases a milk shake. If she had $10.00, how much money will she have left?

6) $6.00   Sandra purchases a deluxe cheeseburger and a cola. What will her change be if she pays $10.00?

7) $1.50   If Janet wanted to buy a hot dog, how much would it cost her?

8) $5.00   What is the total cost of a milk shake and a taco?

9) $5.50   If Jake wanted to buy a milk shake and a deluxe cheeseburger, how much money would he need?

10) $1.50 What is the total cost of an order of French-fries and a cola?

R) Solve.

hot dog = $1.00	cola = $1.00
order of French-fries = $0.50	ice cream cone = $1.00
hamburger = $2.50	milk shake = $2.50
deluxe cheeseburger = $3.50	taco = $2.50

1) $7.00   What is the total cost of a milk shake, a deluxe cheeseburger, and a hot dog?

2) $4.50   What is the total cost of a cola, a taco, and a hot dog?

3) $3.68   What is the total cost of a deluxe cheeseburger if the sales tax is 5%?

4) $1.50   Janet wants to buy an ice cream cone and an order of French-fries. How much will she have to pay?

5) $1.00   What is the total cost of a cola?

6) $6.00   Steven purchases an order of French-fries, an ice cream cone, and a milk shake. What will his change be if he pays $10.00?

7) $3.50   Marcie wants to buy a deluxe cheeseburger. How much will it cost her?

8) $2.62   What is the total cost of a hamburger if the sales tax is five percent?

9) $5.50   Sandra purchases a hot dog, a cola, and a milk shake. How much change will she get back from $10.00?

10) $6.30   What is the total cost of a milk shake and a deluxe cheeseburger if the sales tax is five percent?

S) Solve.

hot dog = $1.50	cola = $1.00
order of French-fries = $0.50	ice cream cone = $1.50
hamburger = $2.00	milk shake = $2.50
deluxe cheeseburger = $3.50	taco = $2.50

1) $1.00 What is the total cost of a cola?

2) $0.50 What is the total cost of an order of French-fries?

3) $2.50 Allan wants to buy an order of French-fries and a hamburger. How much will he have to pay?

4) $4.50 Janet purchases an order of French-fries. What will her change be if she pays $5.00?

5) $4.72 What is the total cost of an order of French-fries, a milk shake, and an ice cream cone if the sales tax is five percent?

6) $3.00 Ellen wants to buy a hot dog and an ice cream cone. How much will she have to pay?

7) $7.50 Brian purchases a taco. If he had $10.00, how much money will he have left?

8) $8.50 Sharon purchases a hot dog. How much change will she get back from $10.00?

9) $7.00 Jackie purchases a cola and a hamburger. If she had $10.00, how much money will she have left?

10) $2.50 What is the total cost of a hot dog and a cola?

T) Solve.

hot dog = $1.00	cola = $1.00
order of French-fries = $1.00	ice cream cone = $1.50
hamburger = $2.00	milk shake = $2.00
deluxe cheeseburger = $3.00	taco = $2.00

1) $6.00 Janet purchases a cola, a milk shake, and an order of French-fries. How much money will she get back if she pays $10.00?

2) $5.50 Audrey purchases a hamburger, an ice cream cone, and a hot dog. What will her change be if she pays $10.00?

3) $3.15 What is the total cost of an order of French-fries, a cola, and a hot dog if there is a 5% sales tax?

4) $1.00 What is the total cost of an order of French-fries?

5) $4.00 If Paul buys a hot dog, what will his change be if he pays $5.00?

6) $1.00 Jennifer wants to buy an order of French-fries. How much will she have to pay?

7) $2.00 What is the total cost of a milk shake?

8) $3.00 Steven wants to buy a hamburger and a cola. How much will it cost him?

9) $3.00 If Donald wanted to buy a deluxe cheeseburger, how much would he have to pay?

10) $3.00 If Jake buys a taco, and if he had $5.00, how much money will he have left?

U) Solve.

hot dog = $1.50	cola = $1.00
order of French-fries = $1.00	ice cream cone = $1.00
hamburger = $2.00	milk shake = $2.50
deluxe cheeseburger = $3.00	taco = $2.00

1) $5.00 If Steven buys an ice cream cone, a taco, and a hamburger, and if he had $10.00, how much money will he have left?

2) $4.50 What is the total cost of a milk shake, an ice cream cone, and an order of French-fries?

3) $4.00 If Sharon wanted to buy an order of French-fries and a deluxe cheeseburger, how much would it cost her?

4) $1.50 Brian wants to buy a hot dog. How much will it cost him?

5) $6.00 What is the total cost of a milk shake, a hot dog, and a hamburger?

6) $1.00 Marin wants to buy a cola. How much will it cost her?

7) $1.00 If Ellen wanted to buy an ice cream cone, how much would she have to pay?

8) $4.00 Allan purchases an order of French-fries. How much change will he get back from $5.00?

9) $3.50 If Jennifer wanted to buy a milk shake and a cola, how much would it cost her?

10) $7.50 Jackie wants to buy a deluxe cheeseburger, a milk shake, and a taco. How much money will she need?

V) Solve.

hot dog = $1.00	cola = $1.00
order of French-fries = $1.00	ice cream cone = $1.00
hamburger = $2.00	milk shake = $2.00
deluxe cheeseburger = $3.50	taco = $2.50

1) $4.72   What is the total cost of a taco and a hamburger if there is a 5% sales tax?

2) $8.00   If Jake buys a cola and an ice cream cone, how much money will he get back if he pays $10.00?

3) $3.50   If Audrey wanted to buy an ice cream cone and a taco, how much would she have to pay?

4) $6.50   Brian purchases a cola and a taco. What will his change be if he pays $10.00?

5) $1.00   If Donald wanted to buy a hot dog, how much would it cost him?

6) $4.50   What is the total cost of an order of French-fries and a deluxe cheeseburger?

7) $3.00   If Amy buys a hamburger, how much change will she get back from $5.00?

8) $1.05   What is the total cost of an ice cream cone if the sales tax is 5%?

9) $3.50   What is the total cost of a taco and a cola?

10) $4.00   What is the total cost of a milk shake, a hot dog, and an order of French-fries?

W) Solve.

hot dog = $1.00	cola = $1.00
order of French-fries = $1.00	ice cream cone = $1.50
hamburger = $2.50	milk shake = $2.00
deluxe cheeseburger = $3.50	taco = $2.50

1) $2.00   If Sharon wanted to buy a cola and an order of French-fries, how much would she have to pay?

2) $6.00   If David wanted to buy a hamburger, a hot dog, and a taco, how much would it cost him?

3) $6.50   If Donald wanted to buy a deluxe cheeseburger, a cola, and a milk shake, how much would he have to pay?

4) $1.50   What is the total cost of an ice cream cone?

5) $5.50   If Ellen wanted to buy a taco, a cola, and a milk shake, how much would she have to pay?

6) $5.00   Jackie purchases a hot dog, a taco, and an ice cream cone. If she had $10.00, how much money will she have left?

7) $5.78   What is the total cost of a cola, an order of French-fries, and a deluxe cheeseburger if there is a five percent sales tax?

8) $5.00   What is the total cost of a hamburger, a hot dog, and an ice cream cone?

9) $1.05   What is the total cost of a cola if the sales tax is 5%?

10) $8.50   If Sandra wanted to buy a hamburger, a deluxe cheeseburger, and a taco, how much money would she need?

X) Solve.

hot dog = $1.00	cola = $1.00
order of French-fries = $0.50	ice cream cone = $1.00
hamburger = $2.50	milk shake = $2.50
deluxe cheeseburger = $3.00	taco = $2.00

1) $6.00   Janet purchases an ice cream cone, a taco, and a cola. If she had $10.00, how much money will she have left?

2) $6.00   If Adam buys a cola, a taco, and a hot dog, how much money will he get back if he pays $10.00?

3) $4.50   What is the total cost of a hamburger, an ice cream cone, and a hot dog?

4) $7.00   Sharon purchases a cola, a hot dog, and an ice cream cone. How much change will she get back from $10.00?

5) $14.50   If Marcie buys a hot dog, a hamburger, and a taco, and if she had $20.00, how much money will she have left?

6) $6.00   Jackie wants to buy a milk shake, a hot dog, and a hamburger. How much will she have to pay?

7) $2.50   Steven purchases a cola, an order of French-fries, and a hot dog. How much change will he get back from $5.00?

8) $8.00   Sandra purchases an ice cream cone and a cola. How much money will she get back if she pays $10.00?

9) $2.10   What is the total cost of a hot dog and an ice cream cone if there is a 5% sales tax?

10) $2.50   What is the total cost of a milk shake?

Y) Solve.

hot dog = $1.50	cola = $1.00
order of French-fries = $1.00	ice cream cone = $1.50
hamburger = $2.00	milk shake = $2.50
deluxe cheeseburger = $3.00	taco = $2.50

1) $7.00   If Adam buys an order of French-fries and a hamburger, how much change will he get back from $10.00?

2) $3.50   Amy wants to buy a cola and a milk shake. How much money will she need?

3) $4.00   Jake wants to buy a cola and a deluxe cheeseburger. How much will he have to pay?

4) $3.00   If Steven buys a hamburger, how much change will he get back from $5.00?

5) $2.50   If Allan wanted to buy a taco, how much money would he need?

6) $7.00   Donald wants to buy a taco, a deluxe cheeseburger, and an ice cream cone. How much will he have to pay?

7) $4.00   If Janet buys a hamburger, an ice cream cone, and a taco, and if she had $10.00, how much money will she have left?

8) $14.00 If Ellen buys a taco, a milk shake, and an order of French-fries, what will her change be if she pays $20.00?

9) $3.15   What is the total cost of a deluxe cheeseburger if the sales tax is five percent?

10) $1.50 David wants to buy a hot dog. How much money will he need?

Z) Solve.

hot dog = $1.00	cola = $1.00
order of French-fries = $0.00	ice cream cone = $1.00
hamburger = $2.00	milk shake = $2.00
deluxe cheeseburger = $3.00	taco = $2.00

1) $7.00 Sharon purchases a deluxe cheeseburger. How much money will she get back if she pays $10.00?

2) $5.00 If Ellen wanted to buy an ice cream cone, a cola, and a deluxe cheeseburger, how much would it cost her?

3) $7.00 If Billy buys a deluxe cheeseburger and an order of French-fries, how much change will he get back from $10.00?

4) $2.10 What is the total cost of a milk shake if there is a 5% sales tax?

5) $2.00 If Marcie wanted to buy a taco, how much would she have to pay?

6) $5.00 Donald wants to buy a taco, a cola, and a hamburger. How much money will he need?

7) $6.00 If Jackie buys a milk shake and a taco, how much change will she get back from $10.00?

8) $4.00 Janet purchases a cola. How much change will she get back from $5.00?

9) $3.00 What is the total cost of an order of French-fries and a deluxe cheeseburger?

10) $2.00 What is the total cost of a hamburger?

AA) Solve.

hot dog = $1.00	cola = $1.00
order of French-fries = $1.00	ice cream cone = $1.00
hamburger = $2.00	milk shake = $2.00
deluxe cheeseburger = $3.00	taco = $2.00

1) $6.00 If Sandra buys a deluxe cheeseburger and an order of French-fries, what will her change be if she pays $10.00?

2) $5.00 Brian wants to buy a taco, an order of French-fries, and a hamburger. How much money will he need?

3) $4.00 If Jackie buys an order of French-fries, a taco, and a deluxe cheeseburger, how much change will she get back from $10.00?

4) $9.00 Amy purchases an ice cream cone. How much change will she get back from $10.00?

5) $4.00 Allan wants to buy a deluxe cheeseburger and a hot dog. How much will it cost him?

6) $3.15 What is the total cost of a cola and a taco if the sales tax is five percent?

7) $3.00 If Steven wanted to buy a taco and an order of French-fries, how much money would he need?

8) $1.00 What is the total cost of a hot dog?

9) $8.00 Ellen purchases a milk shake. What will her change be if she pays $10.00?

10) $5.25 What is the total cost of a milk shake and a deluxe cheeseburger if there is a 5% sales tax?

BB) Solve.

hot dog = $1.00	cola = $1.00
order of French-fries = $0.00	ice cream cone = $2.00
hamburger = $2.00	milk shake = $2.00
deluxe cheeseburger = $3.00	taco = $2.00

1) __$5.25__ What is the total cost of a hot dog, a taco, and a milk shake if the sales tax is 5%?

2) __$4.00__ If Janet buys a cola, how much change will she get back from $5.00?

3) __$14.00__ If Sharon buys a milk shake, a deluxe cheeseburger, and a hot dog, and if she had $20.00, how much money will she have left?

4) __$3.00__ Allan purchases an ice cream cone. How much money will he get back if he pays $5.00?

5) __$5.00__ Amy wants to buy a milk shake, a cola, and a hamburger. How much money will she need?

6) __$3.00__ If Steven buys a hamburger, how much money will he get back if he pays $5.00?

7) __$5.00__ Michele purchases a deluxe cheeseburger and a taco. What will her change be if she pays $10.00?

8) __$5.00__ If David buys a taco and a deluxe cheeseburger, what will his change be if he pays $10.00?

9) __$2.00__ What is the total cost of a taco?

10) __$5.00__ If Ellen wanted to buy a taco, a hamburger, and a hot dog, how much money would she need?

CC) Solve.

hot dog = $1.00	cola = $1.00
order of French-fries = $0.00	ice cream cone = $1.00
hamburger = $2.00	milk shake = $2.00
deluxe cheeseburger = $3.00	taco = $2.00

1) $2.00   What is the total cost of a hamburger?

2) $4.00   Paul purchases a hot dog. What will his change be if he pays $5.00?

3) $3.15   What is the total cost of a hot dog, a cola, and an ice cream cone if the sales tax is 5%?

4) $6.00   Sharon purchases a milk shake, a hamburger, and an order of French-fries. What will her change be if she pays $10.00?

5) $7.00   Audrey purchases a milk shake and a cola. What will her change be if she pays $10.00?

6) $5.00   Adam purchases a milk shake, a hamburger, and a hot dog. How much change will he get back from $10.00?

7) $6.00   If Steven wanted to buy a taco, a milk shake, and a hamburger, how much would he have to pay?

8) $5.00   If Amy buys an order of French-fries, how much money will she get back if she pays $5.00?

9) $4.20   What is the total cost of a taco and a hamburger if there is a 5% sales tax?

10) $14.00   If Michele buys a cola, a deluxe cheeseburger, and a hamburger, what will her change be if she pays $20.00?

DD) Solve.

hot dog = $1.00	cola = $1.00
order of French-fries = $0.00	ice cream cone = $1.00
hamburger = $2.00	milk shake = $2.00
deluxe cheeseburger = $3.00	taco = $2.00

1) $2.10   What is the total cost of an ice cream cone and a cola if the sales tax is 5%?

2) $3.15   What is the total cost of an ice cream cone, a cola, and a hot dog if the sales tax is 5%?

3) $3.00   If Michele wanted to buy a hot dog and a milk shake, how much money would she need?

4) $0.00   What is the total cost of an order of French-fries?

5) $4.00   What is the total cost of an ice cream cone and a deluxe cheeseburger?

6) $2.00   What is the total cost of a milk shake?

7) $5.25   What is the total cost of a taco, a milk shake, and an ice cream cone if there is a five percent sales tax?

8) $4.20   What is the total cost of a hot dog, a cola, and a taco if there is a five percent sales tax?

9) $7.00   If Ellen buys a cola and a taco, and if she had $10.00, how much money will she have left?

10) $3.00   If Marin buys an ice cream cone and a cola, how much change will she get back from $5.00?

EE) Solve.

hot dog = $1.00	cola = $1.00
order of French-fries = $1.00	ice cream cone = $1.00
hamburger = $2.00	milk shake = $2.00
deluxe cheeseburger = $3.00	taco = $2.00

1) $7.00 If Paul wanted to buy a milk shake, a deluxe cheeseburger, and a hamburger, how much money would he need?

2) $5.00 What is the total cost of a taco, a milk shake, and a cola?

3) $4.00 If Janet wanted to buy a hamburger and a taco, how much would it cost her?

4) $7.00 Jackie purchases a cola and a milk shake. How much change will she get back from $10.00?

5) $6.30 What is the total cost of a milk shake, a taco, and a hamburger if the sales tax is 5%?

6) $3.00 What is the total cost of a hamburger and a hot dog?

7) $1.00 Michele wants to buy a cola. How much will she have to pay?

8) $6.00 Jennifer purchases a hot dog, an ice cream cone, and a taco. How much money will she get back if she pays $10.00?

9) $1.00 What is the total cost of an order of French-fries?

10) $3.15 What is the total cost of a hamburger and a cola if there is a five percent sales tax?

FF) Solve.

hot dog = $1.00	cola = $1.00
order of French-fries = $0.00	ice cream cone = $1.00
hamburger = $2.00	milk shake = $2.00
deluxe cheeseburger = $3.00	taco = $2.00

1) $4.00   What is the total cost of a hot dog and a deluxe cheeseburger?

2) $4.20   What is the total cost of a hot dog, an order of French-fries, and a deluxe cheeseburger if there is a five percent sales tax?

3) $6.00   Sharon wants to buy an ice cream cone, a milk shake, and a deluxe cheeseburger. How much will it cost her?

4) $5.00   If Ellen wanted to buy a milk shake, an order of French-fries, and a deluxe cheeseburger, how much money would she need?

5) $2.10   What is the total cost of a hamburger if the sales tax is 5%?

6) $1.05   What is the total cost of a hot dog if there is a 5% sales tax?

7) $6.00   If Amy buys a milk shake and a hamburger, what will her change be if she pays $10.00?

8) $7.00   Marin purchases a milk shake and a cola. If she had $10.00, how much money will she have left?

9) $8.00   David purchases a hot dog, a cola, and an order of French-fries. How much change will he get back from $10.00?

10) $2.00   Adam wants to buy a hot dog, an order of French-fries, and a cola. How much will he have to pay?

GG) Solve.

hot dog = $2.00	cola = $1.00
order of French-fries = $1.00	ice cream cone = $1.00
hamburger = $2.00	milk shake = $2.00
deluxe cheeseburger = $3.00	taco = $2.00

1) $6.00   Donald purchases a milk shake and a hamburger. How much change will he get back from $10.00?

2) $4.00   What is the total cost of a hot dog and a taco?

3) $7.00   If Brian wanted to buy a deluxe cheeseburger, a taco, and a hamburger, how much money would he need?

4) $1.00   Jake wants to buy an order of French-fries. How much will it cost him?

5) $4.20   What is the total cost of an order of French-fries and a deluxe cheeseburger if the sales tax is 5%?

6) $2.00   If Allan wanted to buy a hamburger, how much money would he need?

7) $5.00   What is the total cost of a deluxe cheeseburger, an ice cream cone, and an order of French-fries?

8) $2.00   Marcie wants to buy a taco. How much will she have to pay?

9) $5.00   If Billy buys a cola, a hamburger, and a taco, how much change will he get back from $10.00?

10) $4.00   Steven purchases a cola. How much money will he get back if he pays $5.00?

HH) Solve.

hot dog = $1.00	cola = $1.00
order of French-fries = $0.00	ice cream cone = $1.00
hamburger = $2.00	milk shake = $2.00
deluxe cheeseburger = $3.00	taco = $2.00

1) $5.00 If Sharon buys an order of French-fries, how much money will she get back if she pays $5.00?

2) $7.00 Jackie purchases a milk shake and a hot dog. How much money will she get back if she pays $10.00?

3) $5.00 If Marcie wanted to buy a hamburger, a taco, and an ice cream cone, how much money would she need?

4) $5.00 Janet wants to buy a cola, a taco, and a milk shake. How much will she have to pay?

5) $9.00 Billy purchases an ice cream cone. If he had $10.00, how much money will he have left?

6) $6.00 If Amy buys a hamburger, a cola, and a hot dog, and if she had $10.00, how much money will she have left?

7) $3.00 If Adam buys a cola and a hot dog, how much money will he get back if he pays $5.00?

8) $1.05 What is the total cost of an ice cream cone and an order of French-fries if the sales tax is 5%?

9) $3.15 What is the total cost of an order of French-fries, an ice cream cone, and a milk shake if there is a five percent sales tax?

10) $6.00 Jake purchases a hamburger, a hot dog, and a cola. What will his change be if he pays $10.00?

II) Solve.

hot dog = $1.00	cola = $1.00
order of French-fries = $0.00	ice cream cone = $1.00
hamburger = $2.00	milk shake = $2.00
deluxe cheeseburger = $3.00	taco = $2.00

1) $6.00 What is the total cost of an ice cream cone, a hamburger, and a deluxe cheeseburger?

2) $1.00 What is the total cost of an ice cream cone?

3) $3.00 Donald wants to buy an order of French-fries and a deluxe cheeseburger. How much will he have to pay?

4) $6.30 What is the total cost of a hot dog, a deluxe cheeseburger, and a taco if the sales tax is five percent?

5) $5.00 Janet wants to buy a milk shake, an ice cream cone, and a hamburger. How much will she have to pay?

6) $6.00 If Ellen buys a taco, an ice cream cone, and a cola, and if she had $10.00, how much money will she have left?

7) $7.00 Michele purchases a hot dog and a hamburger. If she had $10.00, how much money will she have left?

8) $3.00 Jake purchases a hamburger and an order of French-fries. If he had $5.00, how much money will he have left?

9) $8.00 If Allan buys an ice cream cone and a hot dog, and if he had $10.00, how much money will he have left?

10) $3.00 If Paul wanted to buy a hamburger and a hot dog, how much money would he need?

JJ) Solve.

hot dog = $1.00	cola = $1.00
order of French-fries = $1.00	ice cream cone = $1.00
hamburger = $2.00	milk shake = $2.00
deluxe cheeseburger = $3.00	taco = $2.00

1) $1.00   What is the total cost of an order of French-fries?

2) $6.00   If Marcie buys a hot dog, a hamburger, and an ice cream cone, and if she had $10.00, how much money will she have left?

3) $4.00   If Audrey wanted to buy an order of French-fries, an ice cream cone, and a hamburger, how much would she have to pay?

4) $9.00   If Ellen buys a cola, how much money will she get back if she pays $10.00?

5) $3.00   What is the total cost of a deluxe cheeseburger?

6) $7.00   If Jackie buys a hamburger and a cola, what will her change be if she pays $10.00?

7) $4.00   Billy purchases a cola. What will his change be if he pays $5.00?

8) $7.00   Michele purchases a cola and a milk shake. What will her change be if she pays $10.00?

9) $3.15   What is the total cost of an order of French-fries, a cola, and an ice cream cone if the sales tax is 5%?

10) $1.05   What is the total cost of an ice cream cone if the sales tax is 5%?

KK) Solve.

hot dog = $1.00	cola = $1.00
order of French-fries = $0.00	ice cream cone = $1.00
hamburger = $2.00	milk shake = $2.00
deluxe cheeseburger = $3.00	taco = $2.00

1) __$5.00__ Marcie wants to buy a milk shake and a deluxe cheeseburger. How much will it cost her?

2) __$4.20__ What is the total cost of an order of French-fries, a cola, and a deluxe cheeseburger if the sales tax is five percent?

3) __$4.00__ Jake purchases a hot dog. How much change will he get back from $5.00?

4) __$2.00__ Adam wants to buy a milk shake. How much money will he need?

5) __$2.00__ What is the total cost of a hamburger?

6) __$13.00__ Jennifer purchases a hamburger, a deluxe cheeseburger, and a taco. How much money will she get back if she pays $20.00?

7) __$6.00__ If Steven buys a milk shake and a hamburger, and if he had $10.00, how much money will he have left?

8) __$3.00__ If Ellen wanted to buy a cola, an ice cream cone, and a hot dog, how much would it cost her?

9) __$7.00__ If Allan buys a hot dog, an ice cream cone, and a cola, what will his change be if he pays $10.00?

10) __$5.00__ If Brian buys an order of French-fries, what will his change be if he pays $5.00?

LL) Solve.

hot dog = $1.00	cola = $1.00
order of French-fries = $0.00	ice cream cone = $1.00
hamburger = $2.00	milk shake = $2.00
deluxe cheeseburger = $3.00	taco = $2.00

1) $3.00   If Brian buys a hamburger, how much change will he get back from $5.00?

2) $4.20   What is the total cost of a hamburger and a taco if there is a 5% sales tax?

3) $7.00   David purchases a deluxe cheeseburger. How much money will he get back if he pays $10.00?

4) $8.00   If Adam buys a hamburger, and if he had $10.00, how much money will he have left?

5) $4.00   If Marin wanted to buy a hot dog and a deluxe cheeseburger, how much would it cost her?

6) $2.00   What is the total cost of an ice cream cone and a hot dog?

7) $3.00   If Audrey wanted to buy a taco, an order of French-fries, and an ice cream cone, how much money would she need?

8) $8.00   Jennifer purchases a taco. How much money will she get back if she pays $10.00?

9) $7.00   If Sharon buys a hot dog, an order of French-fries, and a hamburger, what will her change be if she pays $10.00?

10) $1.05   What is the total cost of a hot dog if there is a 5% sales tax?

MM) Solve.

hot dog = $1.00	cola = $1.00
order of French-fries = $1.00	ice cream cone = $1.00
hamburger = $2.00	milk shake = $2.00
deluxe cheeseburger = $3.00	taco = $2.00

1) $4.00   Amy wants to buy an order of French-fries, an ice cream cone, and a milk shake. How much money will she need?

2) $5.00   If Jake wanted to buy a deluxe cheeseburger and a hamburger, how much would it cost him?

3) $7.00   Ellen purchases a hot dog and a hamburger. How much change will she get back from $10.00?

4) $1.00   What is the total cost of an ice cream cone?

5) $8.00   If Marcie buys an order of French-fries and a cola, what will her change be if she pays $10.00?

6) $7.00   If Adam buys an ice cream cone and a milk shake, how much money will he get back if he pays $10.00?

7) $4.00   If Jackie buys an order of French-fries, how much money will she get back if she pays $5.00?

8) $4.00   If Sharon wanted to buy a hot dog, a hamburger, and an ice cream cone, how much would it cost her?

9) $6.00   If Steven buys a cola and a deluxe cheeseburger, how much change will he get back from $10.00?

10) $3.00   What is the total cost of an ice cream cone, a hot dog, and an order of French-fries?

NN) Solve.

hot dog = $1.00	cola = $1.00
order of French-fries = $1.00	ice cream cone = $1.00
hamburger = $2.00	milk shake = $2.00
deluxe cheeseburger = $3.00	taco = $2.00

1) $14.00   If Sharon buys a deluxe cheeseburger, an order of French-fries, and a hamburger, how much money will she get back if she pays $20.00?

2) $3.00   What is the total cost of a milk shake and a hot dog?

3) $6.90   What is the total cost of an ice cream cone, a taco, and a deluxe cheeseburger if there is a fifteen percent sales tax?

4) $4.00   What is the total cost of a taco and a hamburger?

5) $7.00   Brian purchases an order of French-fries, an ice cream cone, and a cola. What will his change be if he pays $10.00?

6) $2.30   What is the total cost of a taco if the sales tax is 15%?

7) $1.00   If David wanted to buy an order of French-fries, how much would it cost him?

8) $4.60   What is the total cost of a hot dog, an order of French-fries, and a taco if the sales tax is 15%?

9) $3.00   Allan wants to buy a deluxe cheeseburger. How much money will he need?

10) $2.00   If Steven wanted to buy a taco, how much would he have to pay?

OO) Solve.

hot dog = $1.00	cola = $1.00
order of French-fries = $1.00	ice cream cone = $1.00
hamburger = $2.00	milk shake = $2.00
deluxe cheeseburger = $3.00	taco = $2.00

1) $2.00   What is the total cost of a milk shake?

2) $8.00   Marin purchases a milk shake. What will her change be if she pays $10.00?

3) $2.00   Sandra wants to buy a cola and an order of French-fries. How much will she have to pay?

4) $3.00   Allan purchases a milk shake, a deluxe cheeseburger, and a hamburger. What will his change be if he pays $10.00?

5) $3.00   What is the total cost of a hot dog and a milk shake?

6) $5.00   Michele purchases a taco, a cola, and a hamburger. If she had $10.00, how much money will she have left?

7) $4.00   What is the total cost of a cola, an ice cream cone, and a hamburger?

8) $3.00   If Sharon buys a milk shake, and if she had $5.00, how much money will she have left?

9) $7.00   Jennifer purchases an order of French-fries and a taco. What will her change be if she pays $10.00?

10) $2.00   If Steven wanted to buy a cola and a hot dog, how much would it cost him?

PP) Solve.

hot dog = $1.00	cola = $1.00
order of French-fries = $0.00	ice cream cone = $1.00
hamburger = $2.00	milk shake = $2.00
deluxe cheeseburger = $3.00	taco = $2.00

1) $1.00   If Marcie wanted to buy a cola, how much would she have to pay?

2) $3.45   What is the total cost of a milk shake, a hot dog, and an order of French-fries if there is a 15% sales tax?

3) $5.00   What is the total cost of a hamburger and a deluxe cheeseburger?

4) $14.00   If Ellen buys a deluxe cheeseburger, a milk shake, and a hot dog, how much change will she get back from $20.00?

5) $2.30   What is the total cost of a milk shake and an order of French-fries if there is a 15% sales tax?

6) $2.00   Paul wants to buy an ice cream cone, a cola, and an order of French-fries. How much money will he need?

7) $3.00   Allan purchases a hot dog and a cola. How much money will he get back if he pays $5.00?

8) $2.00   What is the total cost of an order of French-fries and a taco?

9) $3.00   What is the total cost of a deluxe cheeseburger?

10) $1.15   What is the total cost of a hot dog if there is a 15% sales tax?

QQ) Solve.

hot dog = $1.00	cola = $1.00
order of French-fries = $1.00	ice cream cone = $1.00
hamburger = $2.00	milk shake = $2.00
deluxe cheeseburger = $3.00	taco = $2.00

1) $3.00   If Audrey wanted to buy a hamburger and an ice cream cone, how much would it cost her?

2) $4.60   What is the total cost of a hamburger, a cola, and a hot dog if the sales tax is fifteen percent?

3) $2.00   Amy wants to buy an order of French-fries and an ice cream cone. How much money will she need?

4) $1.00   What is the total cost of a hot dog?

5) $6.00   Marcie purchases an order of French-fries and a deluxe cheeseburger. How much money will she get back if she pays $10.00?

6) $7.00   If Allan buys an ice cream cone and a milk shake, how much money will he get back if he pays $10.00?

7) $1.00   If Marin wanted to buy a hot dog, how much would it cost her?

8) $3.45   What is the total cost of a deluxe cheeseburger if there is a 15% sales tax?

9) $3.00   Janet purchases a milk shake. How much change will she get back from $5.00?

10) $4.00   What is the total cost of an order of French-fries and a deluxe cheeseburger?

RR) Solve.

hot dog = $1.00	cola = $1.00
order of French-fries = $1.00	ice cream cone = $1.00
hamburger = $2.00	milk shake = $2.00
deluxe cheeseburger = $3.00	taco = $2.00

1) __$6.00__ What is the total cost of a deluxe cheeseburger, an order of French-fries, and a taco?

2) __$5.00__ What is the total cost of a hot dog, a cola, and a deluxe cheeseburger?

3) __$2.00__ What is the total cost of a hamburger?

4) __$4.00__ Jackie purchases a hot dog. How much change will she get back from $5.00?

5) __$5.00__ Jennifer wants to buy a hamburger and a deluxe cheeseburger. How much will it cost her?

6) __$3.00__ If Steven buys a hot dog and an ice cream cone, what will his change be if he pays $5.00?

7) __$1.00__ If Marin wanted to buy a hot dog, how much money would she need?

8) __$4.00__ What is the total cost of a taco, an ice cream cone, and a hot dog?

9) __$3.00__ If Allan wanted to buy a hamburger and an ice cream cone, how much would he have to pay?

10) __$6.00__ If Janet buys a taco and a milk shake, and if she had $10.00, how much money will she have left?

SS) Solve.

hot dog = $1.00	cola = $1.00
order of French-fries = $1.00	ice cream cone = $1.00
hamburger = $2.00	milk shake = $2.00
deluxe cheeseburger = $3.00	taco = $2.00

1) $7.00   If Sandra buys a hot dog and a milk shake, how much change will she get back from $10.00?

2) $4.00   Audrey purchases a hot dog. How much money will she get back if she pays $5.00?

3) $4.00   What is the total cost of an order of French-fries, a hamburger, and a cola?

4) $5.75   What is the total cost of a deluxe cheeseburger and a taco if the sales tax is fifteen percent?

5) $1.00   What is the total cost of an order of French-fries?

6) $4.00   Marin wants to buy a taco and a milk shake. How much will she have to pay?

7) $6.00   Allan wants to buy a hamburger, a deluxe cheeseburger, and an ice cream cone. How much will it cost him?

8) $3.00   If Sharon wanted to buy a taco and an ice cream cone, how much money would she need?

9) $5.00   If Brian buys a milk shake, a hamburger, and an order of French-fries, and if he had $10.00, how much money will he have left?

10) $1.00   If Paul wanted to buy a hot dog, how much would it cost him?

TT) Solve.

hot dog = $1.00	cola = $1.00
order of French-fries = $0.00	ice cream cone = $1.00
hamburger = $2.00	milk shake = $2.00
deluxe cheeseburger = $3.00	taco = $2.00

1) __$9.00__ What is the total cost of four hot dogs and five ice cream cones?

2) __$3.45__ What is the total cost of five orders of French-fries, a milk shake, and a hot dog if there is a 15% sales tax?

3) __$7.00__ Michele purchases three ice cream cones. What will her change be if she pays $10.00?

4) __$1.15__ What is the total cost of an ice cream cone if there is a 15% sales tax?

5) __$8.00__ What is the total cost of a hamburger and three milk shakes?

6) __$10.00__ If Jackie wanted to buy five hamburgers, how much money would she need?

7) __$4.00__ What is the total cost of four ice cream cones?

8) __$7.00__ If Adam buys four milk shakes, what will his change be if he pays $15.00?

9) __$18.00__ If Sharon wanted to buy five milk shakes, three hamburgers, and two hot dogs, how much would she have to pay?

10) __$13.00__ If Steven wanted to buy two deluxe cheeseburgers, four ice cream cones, and three hot dogs, how much money would he need?

UU) Solve.

hot dog = $1.00	cola = $1.00
order of French-fries = $1.00	ice cream cone = $1.00
hamburger = $2.00	milk shake = $2.00
deluxe cheeseburger = $3.00	taco = $2.00

1) $13.00 What is the total cost of three orders of French-fries and five tacos?

2) $5.00   Michele purchases five colas. If she had $10.00, how much money will she have left?

3) $22.00 What is the total cost of five hamburgers and four deluxe cheeseburgers?

4) $19.55 What is the total cost of three hot dogs, three hamburgers, and four tacos if there is a 15% sales tax?

5) $6.90   What is the total cost of three tacos if there is a 15% sales tax?

6) $8.00   If Amy buys a milk shake, what will her change be if she pays $10.00?

7) $6.00   If Jake buys a hamburger and two ice cream cones, what will his change be if he pays $10.00?

8) $2.30   What is the total cost of two ice cream cones if the sales tax is fifteen percent?

9) $11.50 What is the total cost of five hamburgers if the sales tax is fifteen percent?

10) $10.00 David wants to buy an ice cream cone, four tacos, and a cola. How much money will he need?

VV) Solve.

hot dog = $1.00	cola = $1.00
order of French-fries = $1.00	ice cream cone = $1.00
hamburger = $2.00	milk shake = $2.00
deluxe cheeseburger = $3.00	taco = $2.00

1) $20.00   Allan wants to buy four hot dogs, five hamburgers, and two deluxe cheeseburgers. How much money will he need?

2) $21.85   What is the total cost of five deluxe cheeseburgers and four colas if the sales tax is fifteen percent?

3) $6.00   What is the total cost of three hamburgers?

4) $5.00   If Sandra wanted to buy three orders of French-fries and a milk shake, how much money would she need?

5) $2.00   If Audrey wanted to buy a taco, how much money would she need?

6) $1.00   What is the total cost of a cola?

7) $2.00   What is the total cost of two ice cream cones?

8) $4.00   Janet wants to buy four ice cream cones. How much will she have to pay?

9) $8.00   Ellen purchases a taco. If she had $10.00, how much money will she have left?

10) $21.00   If Paul wanted to buy five deluxe cheeseburgers, two tacos, and two colas, how much would he have to pay?

WW) Solve.

hot dog = $1.00	cola = $1.00
order of French-fries = $1.00	ice cream cone = $1.00
hamburger = $2.00	milk shake = $2.00
deluxe cheeseburger = $3.00	taco = $2.00

1) $16.00   What is the total cost of five hot dogs, three colas, and four tacos?

2) $15.00   Marcie purchases two orders of French-fries, four ice cream cones, and three deluxe cheeseburgers. How much money will she get back if she pays $30.00?

3) $6.00   Jake purchases four colas and five milk shakes. How much change will he get back from $20.00?

4) $15.00   Allan wants to buy three ice cream cones, three hamburgers, and three tacos. How much money will he need?

5) $4.60   What is the total cost of two milk shakes if the sales tax is 15%?

6) $12.00   If Billy wanted to buy two ice cream cones and five milk shakes, how much would it cost him?

7) $9.00   Sandra purchases a cola. If she had $10.00, how much money will she have left?

8) $14.95   What is the total cost of four orders of French-fries, three hot dogs, and three hamburgers if the sales tax is 15%?

9) $18.00   If Janet wanted to buy three hamburgers, three orders of French-fries, and three deluxe cheeseburgers, how much money would she need?

10) $14.00   Jennifer purchases five milk shakes, two hot dogs, and two hamburgers. How much change will she get back from $30.00?

XX) Solve.

hot dog = $1.00	cola = $1.00
order of French-fries = $1.00	ice cream cone = $1.00
hamburger = $2.00	milk shake = $2.00
deluxe cheeseburger = $3.00	taco = $2.00

1) $5.00   Audrey purchases five hot dogs. If she had $10.00, how much money will she have left?

2) $25.30 What is the total cost of five deluxe cheeseburgers, four ice cream cones, and three colas if the sales tax is fifteen percent?

3) $6.90   What is the total cost of three milk shakes if the sales tax is fifteen percent?

4) $13.80 What is the total cost of a deluxe cheeseburger, three milk shakes, and three hot dogs if there is a fifteen percent sales tax?

5) $2.00   If Steven wanted to buy a hamburger, how much would it cost him?

6) $3.00   Allan purchases three milk shakes, two tacos, and two ice cream cones. How much change will he get back from $15.00?

7) $6.00   If Michele buys two hamburgers, and if she had $10.00, how much money will she have left?

8) $15.00 Jennifer purchases three tacos, five orders of French-fries, and four hot dogs. If she had $30.00, how much money will she have left?

9) $11.00 Jake purchases two deluxe cheeseburgers, five milk shakes, and three hot dogs. If he had $30.00, how much money will he have left?

10) $1.00 Amy wants to buy a hot dog. How much will she have to pay?

Made in the USA
Las Vegas, NV
08 January 2024